CONTENTS

Illustrations

Chapter 1

BUDGET CHALLENGES

That we are in the midst of crisis is now well understood. Our nation is at war against a far-reaching network of violence and hatred. Our economy is badly weakened, a consequence of greed and irresponsibility on the part of some, but also our collective failure to make hard choices and prepare the nation for a new age. Homes have been lost, jobs shed, businesses shuttered. Our health care is too costly, our schools fail too many – and each day brings further evidence that the ways we use energy strengthen our adversaries and threaten our planet.

-- President Barack Hussein Obama

Political administrations must annually surmount challenges and endure debates regarding the allocation of taxpayer funds; the challenge lies in the balancing of federal budget priorities. The debate, as often constructed, is a choice between guns and butter— national security versus economic prosperity. President Obama, during his inaugural address, clearly stated the United States is in a crisis involving both the national security and economic well-being of the country.[1] Even though there seems to be two choices, funding decisions are not binary in nature; the balance between the two objectives is more than a sliding scale between national security and economic prosperity; the desire for both actually facilitates each other. The purchase of defense equipment does stimulate the economy while a strong economy makes possible the purchase of defense equipment.[2] However, there is a unknown risk if the nation allocates too little funding to the defense side of the ledger. As a leading strategist wrote, "Heavy defense expenditure may damage the economy, but inadequate defense expenditure assuredly will imperil the physical security of the country, as well as the health of the economy. A sound economy

---

[1] White House, "Obama's State of the Union Address, 2009," http://www.whitehouse.gov/the_press_office/remarks-of-President -Barack-Obama-Address-to-Joint-Session-of-Congress/ (accessed 5 March 2009)

[2] Martin Feldstein, "The Economic Stimulus and Sustained Economic Growth," *Full Statement for the House Democratic Steering and Policy Committee,* 7 January 2009. Mr. Feldstein recommended increased spending in the defense sector and was surprised the economic stimulus bill did not contain funding for defense projects…thoughts are rooted to theories developed during the 1950s supporting large defense budgets to support the economy.

is no guarantor of security."[3] However, the issues remain. How much funding should an administration allocate to defense spending?

The debate and decisions regarding defense fund allocation appear straightforward in periods of relative certainty. During an open conflict, the nation recognizes the threats, political leaders generally grasp the stakes involved, and as a result, administrations will not accept the major risks inherent in shortchanging the war machine.[4] The debate and funding decisions tilt towards guns during periods of open conflict; the nation is willing to mortgage the country to win the war. Wars, as a result, tend to drive deficit spending no matter how prudent the administration; the risks of losing the war outweigh the costs and risks of incurring debt.[5] As the war terminates, the deficits snap the government's focus back to the economy as the nation, normally, drastically reduces defense spending, quickly demobilizes the force structure, and forces the services to use leftover equipment in preparation for a future war. The end of the war implies an end to hostilities and a lasting peace. Politicians can reprioritize the objective of national security with economic prosperity, and focus on protection against inflation, recession, and high unemployment rates.

A stable and predictable geopolitical environment simplifies the budget challenge as the choices seem clearer during times of war and peace. As the experienced strategist is aware, however, the geopolitical environment is never straightforward or clear. The growing complexity of the world economy, its transformation via the information superhighway and globalization, and further third world development challenges create friction and cast additional fog around the strategist. The budget challenges increase in difficulty due to an uncertain and complex world. It is within this complex and uncertain environment that politicians and strategists apply their art.

An important aspect of the strategist's job, within this construct, is to examine the means at hand and determine the best use of the means to accomplish the political goals or achieve the desired political end-state. The broad political goals, as used within this thesis, are achieving national security and economic prosperity. The challenge is

---

[3] Colin S. Gray, *Explorations in Strategy* (Westport, CT: Praeger Publishers, 1996), 115.
[4] Robert D. Hormats, *The Price of Liberty* (New York: Times Books, 2007). Hormats documents the nation's history of raising the funds necessary to fight the nation's wars.
[5] Hormats, *The Price of Liberty.* Hormats documents the nation's early history of raising funds for the military in times of war, and following the conflict, seeking taxing methods to pay off debts.

determining the method of allocating funding to ensure the nation has the right and proper mix of means. Colin Gray, one of the today's recognized experts on strategy, defines strategy in a manner useful for understanding the role of budgets. For Gray, strategy is the bridge linking means with political end states or objectives.[6] In other words, budgets purchase and maintain the means available to achieve political goals and the means available will determine whether the bridge is a simple rope path, a covered wooden bridge or as complex as the Golden Gate Bridge.

The need to maintain a continuous advantage further complicates the strategist's problem. This position of advantage can be applied within both of the nation's objectives of security and prosperity. The idea of a continuous advantage, as it relates to strategy, is taken from the writings of Dr. Everett Dolman. [7] In his book *Pure Strategy*, Dolman observed that strategy "is about the future, and above all it is about change. It is anticipation of the probable and preparation for the possible. It is, in a word, alchemy; a method of transmutation from idea into action."[8] These concepts fit nicely into our dynamic, complex, and uncertain world; in fact, Dolman explicitly addressed the complexity that exists, describing the world as "unfathomably intricate" and that no matter the "effort to account for all possible events, there is at least one more we could not have accounted for."[9] The good alchemist or strategist develops a strategy leading "to a strong probability of recurring or continuing advantage."[10] Linked to developing a strategy providing a continuous advantage, the means must be useful, adaptive, and provide multiple solutions. The strategist and politician must understand the capabilities of the means purchased with yesteryears' budgets, examine the current and future elements in the national security and economic arenas, and build tomorrow's budgets to maintain the advantage by filling in the gaps.

There are additional difficulties facing today's strategist. Prior to the advent of flight, the United States, within the national security realm, focused on two war domains – sea

---

[6] Colin S. Gray, *Fighting Talk: Forty Maxims on War, Peace and Strategy* (Westport, CT: Praeger Publishers, 2007), 55.

[7] Dr. Everett C. Dolman specializes in space theory, is the author of *Astropolitik: Classical Geopolitics in the Space Age,* and serves as a professor at the Air Force's School of Advance Air and Space Studies.

[8] Everett C. Dolman, *Pure Strategy: Power and Principle in the Space and Information Age* (London: Frank Cass, 2005), 1.

[9] Dolman, *Pure Strategy*, 12-13.

[10] Dolman, *Pure Strategy*, 12.

and land. Today's strategist must consider "five geographically distinctive dimensions of war…and the nuclear wildcard."[11] These domains include sea, land, air, space, and now cyberspace.

Within the economic arena, the challenges are increasing as the movement from production industries to high-tech-service-related industries requires a greater level of education, increase in the globalized marketplace requires a global approach, and environmental pressures act to constrain expansion, to name a few. All of these challenges increase the complexity and uncertainness faced by the strategist. Given this complexity, one must accept the fact that strategies and budget decisions will not be perfect. As Dr. Gray wrote, "it is obvious that there can be no demonstrably right strategy and force structure for the future. Instead, the charge has to be a search for strategy and force structure 'right enough' that should be tolerant of inevitable errors."[12] Although the strategist may be daunted by the demands required, she must operate and develop strategies ensuring national security and economic prosperity within this dynamic environment.

The United States is currently operating within that dynamic, complex, and uncertain environment. President Obama's administration faces a myriad of challenges from both an economic and national security aspect. Numerous imminent economic failures to include the failure of several national banks, the bankruptcy of America's traditional economic engine General Motors, and a steep increase in housing foreclosures challenge the administration. All of these threats are driving unemployment rates, business closures, and financial market indices to historical 25-year negative levels. The national debt is expected to triple over the next ten years, while reaching a $1.75 trillion deficit level in 2010.[13] Against this backdrop, the nation's military continues to be involved in a worldwide struggle against international terrorism. The United States is carrying out major operations in Iraq and Afghanistan, while conducting additional operations in Africa, the Philippines, and South America, while at the same time maintaining a presence in Western Europe and South Korea.

---

[11] Gray, *Explorations in Strategy*, xiv.
[12] Gray, *Explorations in Strategy*, 112.
[13] Rebecca Christie, "Geithner Tells China U.S. Will Tackle Budget Deficit," *Bloomberg,* 1 June 2009, http://www.bloomberg.com/apps/news?pid=20601087&sid=aFaYiMwPZyq0&refer=home (accessed 1 June 2009).

The new administration was going to be challenged by the federal budget, defense funding in particular, whether or not the economy was in decline; the worsening economy has simply sharpened the debate and exasperate the challenges. Key leaders within the House of Representatives have warned the military services to prepare for decreasing military budgets. Congressman Murtha, chairperson of the powerful House Appropriations Committee on Defense, stated in December of 2008, "Our job will be to manage the current and future threats under a constrained defense budget."[14] In his keynote speech to the Center for American Progress, Murtha laid out the "enormity of the challenges," by documenting the history of defense spending during and following engagements such as Vietnam and the Cold War, focusing on the sharp decreases in funding, and listing the status of the means available to design a national security strategy for tomorrow's threats, complex environment and constrained budgets.[15]

Congressional leaders are not the only voices sounding the alarm regarding defense budget cuts. Various experts from think tanks and watchdog groups have predicted defense-funding streams to run dry as the wars in Iraq and Afghanistan end. Dr Ashton Carter, co-director of the Preventive Defense Project and recently confirmed as the next Undersecretary for Acquisition, Technology and Logistics, addresses what he calls "The strategy-resources mismatch" the new administration will face.[16] Carter points to the fact that defense budgets cannot continue to grow at current rates and with the continuing price increase of defense programs, making the problem even more daunting. The Center for Arms Control and Non-Proliferation also predicts defense-spending cuts, but stated there is a positive aspect within the crisis in that the budget crisis will allow for acquisition reform, the cancelation of high-tech weapon programs, and development and adoption of more cost effective strategies.[17] Lastly, Defense Secretary Gates has also

---

[14] Representative John Murtha, "Murtha Delivers Keynote Speech on Military Spending and Challenges Facing the Incoming Obama Administration," Murtha's Press Release, 10 December 2008, http://www.murtha.house.gov/index.php?.option=com_content&task=view&id=576 (accessed 22 March 2009).

[15] Murtha, "Murtha Delivers Keynote Speech,"1.

[16] Ashton B. Carter, "Defense Strategy & Budget in the Post-Bush Era," (paper, Aspen Strategy Group: 5 August 2008) http://belfercenter ksg harvard.edu/publication/18521/defense_strategy_budget_in_the_post_bush_era (accessed 9 November 2008).

[17] Travis Sharp, "Pentagon Budgets Faces Uncertain Future," *Center for Arms Control and Non-Proliferation,* 3 February 2009, www.armscontrolcenter.org (accessed 12 February 2009).

called attention to forthcoming cuts in the defense budgets, while during a hearing before the Senate Armed Services Committee in early 2009, Secretary Gates stated, "The spigot of defense spending that opened on September 11 is closing."[18] While it appears the Obama administration is facing serious problems, today's challenges are not new or unique.

The Obama administration can find answers or lessons for the current debate by studying America's history. While these problems seem daunting and overwhelming, the nation has experienced similar situations in its short history that could provide a tutorial. The Truman and George H.W. Bush administrations each faced complex and uncertain environments early within their terms. President Truman had to navigate the United States through the end of World War II, the advent of the atomic age, the economy's conversion from a defensive to domestic focus while controlling inflation and unemployment, and creating a stable post-war geopolitical environment. Truman faced record debt levels, the conclusion of a two front war, a world in economic shambles due to the ravages of war, and an uncertain threat environment. While Truman set the nation's policy as it entered the Cold War, Bush had to reset the course with the fall of the Iron Curtain and the end of the Cold War. The Bush administration had to address record debt levels, an uncertain threat environment due to the loss of a bi-polar world, the economic hardships of Eastern Europe, the beginning of a national recession, and the hard push to realize a peace dividend.

Each of these administrations faced the challenges of balancing funding allocations between national security and domestic programs. Each president guided the country through the end of a major engagement into a hopeful new geopolitical world of peace. President Truman followed through on the creation of the United Nations while President Bush's administration called for a New World Order. Within each of these administrations, the geopolitical threats and risks were uncertain, and each embraced the

---

[18] Shaun Waterman, "Budget Analysts Warn of Spiraling Defense Spending," *Washington Times*, 12 February 2009, http://ebird.osd.mil/ebfiles/e20090212656650 html (accessed 12 February 2009).

hope for a better tomorrow. Through President Barack Obama's speeches and press releases, one can trace many policy parallels to these previous administrations.[19]

The purpose of this thesis is to examine those policy parallels and review how the economy, threats, strategy, and the nation's cultural norms influenced the respective administration decisions regarding the defense budget. By identifying the motivators, the strategist can understand the influences and context of past decisions and in order to understand better the impact of decisions on the geopolitical and economic landscape, and implications for the future.

The thesis is divided into five chapters. While this chapter frames the question and purpose of the thesis, the remaining four provide case studies, definitions, historical constructs, models, issues, and a framework for future challenges. In the next chapter, the reader will gain an understanding of the various methods in formulating budgets as well as an historical review of defense funding allocation within the United States prior to World War II. Chapters three and four consist of case studies, focusing on the Truman and Bush administrations. These chapters will pay particular attention to how the nation's history, threats, economic conditions, and strategic goals influenced budget decisions. Finally, the last chapter will draw conclusions and lessons from the case studies applicable for the Obama administration.

Even though there was debate regarding the America's cultural norms during the nation's early history, the United States exhibited the cultural norms of distrusting a standing military, avoiding foreign alliances, and minimizing national debt in determining the nation's national security policy. The following chapter provides a review of how these factors influenced the nation's decisions. In addition to this historical review, the chapter will examine the four budgeting methods that will serve as our lenses for the subsequent case studies.

---

[19] White House, "Obama's State of the Union Address, 2009," http://www.whitehouse.gov/the_press_office/remarks-of-President -Barack-Obama-Address-to-Joint-Session-of-Congress/ (accessed 5 March 2009)

Chapter 2

BUDGET FORMULATION METHODS

Over the centuries emperors, kings, princes, and democratic governments have pondered...how to have an armed force available to advance and protect the interests, at an affordable financial and political cost, and in such a way that it does not threaten them.

-- General Rupert Smith

The most economical and efficient peace-time policy of defense is one that provides: (1) The minimum necessary for an active establishment, maintained in the highest state of efficiency (personnel and material) and immediately available for active service; (2) a war reserve sufficient for its purposes; (3) and comprehensive measures of preparation for mobilization of the National effort. To neglect the active establishment, the war reserve, or the provisions for mobilizing the Nation, would be a blunder that might prove fatal.

-- General Douglas McArthur

A myriad of questions surround the formulation of defense budgets. How much should a nation spend on defense? What factors should drive the decision? Should one base the decision on striking a balance between national security and domestic programs? Can the defense budget be set at a level to counter likely security threats? Should the defense budget be set at what is affordable or what is available after funding domestic priorities? Should the nation tie the defense budget to its security strategy? Annually, the problem of balancing limited resources and ensuring the nation's security confronts the government. Each administration must consider a range of economic conditions, threats, and geopolitical goals. The economic conditions can range from the lows of the Great Depression to the heights of economic prosperity experienced during the 1950s. The nation can experience the threat of elimination due to nuclear war or peripheral risks such as Indian raids along the frontier. The country's geopolitical goals can be as simple as avoiding foreign alliances and entanglements, or escalate to policing the world and promoting stable, democratic governments. Each factor plays its part determining the size of the defense budget. The influence of each issue varies based on the environmental context.

This chapter will examine the historical ebb and flow of defense budgets and force structures from the Revolutionary War to the beginning of World War II as well as review the various defense budget methods offered in the literature. By reviewing the nations' first 150 years, the reader will gain an understanding of America's reluctance to support a large standing army or fund sizeable military budgets. Each of the factors identified above influenced the nation's choices; the benefits and the costs of these decisions vary depending on the analyst's perspective. Following the historical analysis, the chapter will review four budget formulation models to include the historical-based, threat-based, economy-based, and strategy-based models. These models will be used as the lenses to examine the Truman and Bush administrations' efforts in formulating defense budgets at the end of major conflicts in the following chapters.

The Nation's Cultural Norm

Throughout the early history of the United States, the factors and processes establishing the defense budget varied little. The United States had an historical tendency to sharply reduce defense budgets and dramatically demobilize force structure at the end of wars. This tendency was rooted in the nation's historical distrust of a standing army.[1] As stated by a nineteenth century military historian, "[o]ur military policy has been largely shaped by the Anglo-Saxon prejudice against "standing armies as a dangerous menace to liberty."[2] In addition to this distrust, the nation was driven to eliminate debt and budget deficits, and struggled in devising means to raise revenue and capital.[3] Because of this combination, Congress disbanded the army at the end of the Revolutionary War due to financial concerns as the war had resulted in "the finances of the nation being completely exhausted."[4] This proclivity to maintain balanced budgets and avoid personal taxes strengthened the case for small standing armies. The nation repeated this behavior of cutting funds and demobilizing forces at the end of conflicts throughout its early history. In table 1, one can examine the ebb and flow of force structure, and how quickly Congress acted to demobilize the army.

---

[1] See Emory Upton, *Military Policy of the United States:* Charles A. Stevenson, *Congress at War,* 35; John Stevenson, *Congress At War*, 35; David Johnson, *Fast Tanks and Heavy Bombers,*29; *The Hoover Commission Report,185;* —each documents concept of the United States distrusted standing armies.
[2] Brevet Maj Gen Emory Upton, *The Military Policy of the United States* (Washington: War Dept, 1912), IX.
[3] Robert D. Hormats, *The Price of Liberty* (New York: Times Books, Henry Holt & Company, 2007), xiv.
[4] Upton, *Military Policy of the US*, 68.

Table 1: Force Mobilization and Demobilization during National Conflicts (1775 – 1945)

War	Beginning Force Level	Peak Force Level	Drawdown Force Level	Congressional Directed Reduction	National Debt
Revolutionary (1775 – 1783)	0	231,771	800	1784	$75M
War of 1812 (1812 – 1815)	5,608	38,186	10,231	1815	$127M
Florida War (1835 –1842)	4,000	12,539	9,102	1842	$20M
Mexican War (1846 –1848)	8,409	47,319	10,744	1848	$63M
Civil War (1861 – 1865)	16,215	1,000,692	57,072	1866	$2,773M
Spanish War (1898—1903)	27,375	209,714	69,595	1903	$2,202M
World War I (1917 – 1918)	108,399	2,395,742	204,292	1920	$27,390M
World War II (1941- 1945)	269,023	8,267,958	1,891,011	1945	$258,682M

Complied from various sources: Upton, *Military Policy of the US.* United States, Bureau of Census, *Historical Statistics of the United States, Colonial Times to 1970,*1142. United States Treasury Department, "National Debt Historical Charts," http://www.treasurydirect.gov/govt/reports/pd/histdebt/histdebt htm. Force levels and Congressional action sourced from Upton and Census Bureau documents. National debt levels sourced from Treasury web site.

The War of 1812 is a case in point. The professional army was only 5,000 strong as the nation prepared for war. Congress acted to increase the force size as the war neared, yet Congress still expected the militia to carry the heavy load. This behavior is reflected in the fact that the professional army consisted of 15,000 regulars within a total force of 65,000 by the end of 1812.[5] Only after repeated defeats did Congress expand the size of the regular army that finally resulted in a total professional army of 38,000. Congress would not allow this sized force to exist for long. Following the victory at New Orleans, Congress passed a bill reducing the regular army to 10,000, and while the ending professional force was a two-fold increase from the 5,000 originally defending the nation, Congress would whittle away at this professional army over the next 10 years.[6]

The reorganization of the Army in 1821 illuminated Congress' continuing concern regarding a standing army and national debt. Since the War of 1812, the United

[5] Upton, *Military Policy of the US*, 105, 137. United States, Bureau of Census, *Historical Statistics of the United States, Colonial Times to 1970* (Washington, DC: Government Printing Office, 1975), 1142.
[6] Upton, *Military Policy of the US,* 143-149.

States had only faced one limited engagement against Indians in Florida; the Seminole War occurred in 1817, and the conflict was over in three months. Following the conflict, the nation enjoyed relative peace along the frontier allowing Congress, in 1821, to reduce the strength of the Army from 12,000 to 6,000.[7] These cuts reduced the federal budget, allowing the nation to address the national debt of $81 million.[8] The nation's distrust of standing armies coupled with its drive to reduce the nation's debt seemed to outweigh concerns regarding potential threats posed by European powers or American Indians.

The nation would continue its policy of mobilizing and demobilizing; only quickening the demobilization process. By the time of the Florida War in 1835, the nation had reduced the regular military force again from 6,000 to just 4,000 troops.[9] The Florida War would repeat the trend of previous wars, with a buildup of forces due to military defeats, followed with quick demobilization as the conflict terminated. Just nine days after the end of hostilities in the Florida War, Congress cut the army's size in half, beating the four months required to cut the nation's military following the War of 1812. Congress again increased the speed of demobilization during the Mexican War by linking the actual legislation that authorized the regular force increase with a provision reducing the regular force level "when the exigency requiring the increase should cease."[10] Congress linked the demobilization of forces to the peace treaty and made the reduction automatic. The experiences of the Civil War, and Spanish-American War would be little different.

World War I would serve as a special case in that the nation, in particular Congress, began to realize the military policies of the United States were not as effective as needed to fight the nation's wars. As was to be expected, the nation clung to its tradition of avoiding foreign entanglements and enjoying the perceived benefits of isolation, and was reluctant to engage in the war on the European continent. Congress, during the first years of the war, did very little in terms of funding to prepare the nation. This was due to public sentiment, the nation's steady foreign policy of avoiding alliances,

---

[7] Upton, *Military Policy of the US*, 149-150.
[8] United States Treasury Department, "National Debt Historical Charts," http://www.treasurydirect.gov/govt/reports/pd/histdebt/histdebt.htm.
[9] Upton, *Military Policy of the US*, 162-193.
[10] Upton, *Military Policy of the US*, 204.

the continued distrust of standing armies, and funding considerations. Once it entered the war, the nation found itself, as to be expected, unprepared.

The nation had to mobilize forces, purchase equipment, retool industry, and reshape the economy. In order to support its allies, the United States needed to provide well-equipped, professional soldiers, and serve as the industrial engine producing the new instruments of war. These new instruments included the tank and the airplane. However, the nation did not live up to its promises; the United States could not deliver tanks or aircraft in time for the war.[11] Additionally, the army was not able to quickly mobilize and train a professional army; the mobilization of forces was difficult and costly. The allies would win the war, but possibly at a greater cost than was necessary. The results of America's efforts were a wake-up call for Congress; the threats and forms of war had changed and the United States needed to adjust its military policies.

Congress, recognizing a need for change, amended the National Defense Act on June 4, 1920. The Secretary of War stated in his 1921 annual report that Congress had finally recognized the need for a "permanent military policy commensurate with their great potential requirements for national defense, and yet thoroughly consistent with their national traditions."[12] Among the amendment's changes, two stood out. In one of the amendments' primary, Congress granted the executive branch authority over the organization of the Army. The Army could change its structure and focus on creating an organization that could mobilize the nation quickly. The primary lesson gleaned by the Army from World War I was the need for quick mobilization. The Secretary expounded on this theme by stating, "The American people can now, in time of need, be guided in their mobilization through a system prepared by this department in accordance with the best of military doctrine."[13] The solution was not a larger peacetime force structure—it was a process to mobilize the force structure needed for war.

Secondly, the National Defense Act amendment addressed the army's force size. Before Congress debated the act, Army leaders had requested a standing force of 500,000. Due to several factors, including Gen Pershing's force size recommendation

---

[11] David E. Johnson, *Fast Tanks and Heavy Bombers: Innovation in the U.S. Army 1917 – 1945* (London: Cornell University Press, 1998), 22-29.

[12] Department of War, *Report of the Secretary of War to the President, 1921* (Washington: Government Printing Office, 1921), 8.

[13] Department of War, *Report of the Secretary of War to the President, 1921*, 8.

and a Republican controlled Congress calling for budget cuts, the Army was authorized an end strength just short of 300,000.[14] Even though this was an increase from previous force levels, the army would not achieve this force size during the interwar period. The Congress, as in previous eras, continued to downsize the Army from a high of 847,000 in World War I to 202,000 by 1920.[15] The regular army would drop to below 134,000 by 1927. During the interwar period, the size of troop numbers stayed relatively stable at around 135,000.[16] These cuts, during the 1920s, occurred against a backdrop of increased demand for force structure; in particular, occupation forces throughout the Pacific to include the Philippines. Bottom line, the force size was far short of the Army's request of 500,000.

The funding of new equipment also suffered.[17] While other nations developed tanks, aircraft, and other technological innovations, the United States forced the army to use leftover equipment from WWI to train and prepare for the next war.[18] The nation reverted to its historical tendencies with the nation and its politicians maintaining confidence "in oceans as bulwarks and a belief that the Navy could safely be thought of not merely as the traditional 'first line of defense' but as the only real necessary line of defense for the time being."[19] The nation was focused on a defensive posture. The United States did not want to be lured once again into a European War, and these continuing policies would handicap the United States' entry into World War II.

Martin Blumenson, in an essay written for the book *America's First Battles: 1776 – 1965*, states that as World War II began, "the U.S. Army lacked the capacity to wage modern warfare."[20] The causes were, as Blumenson observed, "A revulsion against war in general and disillusionment with WWI in particular," and confidence "in the oceans as

---

[14] Johnson, *Fast Tanks and Heavy Bombers*, 28.

[15] United States, Bureau of Census, *Historical Statistics of the United States, Colonial Times to 1970, Vol 2, (*New York: Basic Books, 1976), 1141.

[16] Mark S Watson, *Chief of Staff Prewar Plans and Preparations US Army in WWII*, (Washington, DC: Department of the Army, 1950), 15.

[17] Watson, *Chief of Staff Prewar*, 15. David E. Johnson, *Fast Tanks and Heavy Bombers,* 66-67.

[18] Johnson, *Fast Tanks and Heavy Bombers*, 66-68. Johnson documents President Harding's military policies of focusing on the economy, need for a small, expandable army, voluntary reserve training and disarmament.

[19] Watson, *Chief of Staff Prewar*, 15.

[20] Charles Heller and William Stofft, ed., *America's First Battles: 1776 – 1965* (Lawrence, KS: University Press of Kansas, 1986), 226.

bulwarks of protection" drove the nation into isolationism.[21] The depression of the 1930s only furthered the problem resulting in fewer dollars being appropriated for development and procurement of weapons and equipment. This short paragraph encapsulates the impact of Congressional policies, funding restrictions, and isolationism on the United States' military force structure and funding.

Did the United States' cultural proclivity for small armies and balanced budgets result in failure? Were any wars lost? On the other hand, could the nation have spent less maintaining a large standing army, thereby shortening its wars? The following analysis addresses these questions.

General Emory Upton's second publication, *The Military Policy of the United States* directed its attention on the nation's ability to raise, train, and prepare an army for war. In his view, the nation was ill prepared for wars due to its cultural desire to maintain a small, regular army while relying on state militias to endure most of the early fighting. He documented and sustained his statements by reviewing the conduct and experiences of the nation's conflicts from the Revolutionary to the Civil War. Upton reviewed the army's performance during both times of conflict and interwar periods. He paid particular attention to the ability of the army to prepare for the next war, the progress of each campaign, and the impact of Congressional policy. More importantly for our purposes, Upton reviewed the national policies at the conclusion of each war and their impact on the military structure and defense funding.

Upton believed, and was influenced, by a Prussian view that war was a recurring theme in man's history and therefore the nation had to be prepared. Upton's first publication was a review of the Civil War and European armies, and during his time in Europe, Upton examined the Prussian military model and the policies and theories of Helmuth von Moltke the Elder. Moltke was the Prussian Chief of Staff during the late 1800s and history credits him with the quick Prussian victories against Austria and France. Moltke's theories and writings influenced Upton regarding the latter's thoughts about the need for a standing army.[22] Several times within his writings, Moltke stated

---

[21] Heller and Stofft, *America's First Battles*, 226.
[22] Upton, *Military Policies, IX.* Upton mentions Moltke in the introduction of his book by stating "while Von Moltke alone made it possible by destroying in two campaigns the military power of Austria and France."

that war was inevitable, writing "Eternal peace is a dream, and not even a pleasant one. War is a part of God's world order."[23] Upton wrote regarding the number of years the United States had been at war stating, "since the publication of the Declaration of Independence to this time these figures show that for every three years of peace we have had one year of actual war."[24] Given the nation was at war 25 percent of the time, war was a natural condition of the nation and the nation needed a larger, professional standing army.

Upton made the case that the dollars saved by maintaining a small, unsuitable army during times of peace were wasted by the loss of material and men at the onslaught of war. More importantly, these policies and budget restrictions prolonged the wars; therefore, it was cheaper, economically, to maintain a strong standing army. He laid the blame for maintaining a small army on Congress bemoaning the fact that those in Congress lacked military expertise. His primary complaint was that the nation spent undue time, resources, and lives during the first stages of each conflict. If the United States had a strong, standing army, the nation could have ended each of its conflicts quickly and the nation would not have suffered defeat at Blandensburg during the War of 1812, would have quickly defeated the Seminoles in Florida, and would have ended the Civil War at the first battle of Bull Run. A larger force structure might even have deterred some of the wars before they began. Instead, the military policies resulted in the nation suffering during the building of a larger regular army while untrained and undisciplined militia fought the initial battles. Moltke provided justification for Upton's main thesis stating, "The best pledge for peace is to be armed for war"[25] and "the better organized our fighting force on land and sea, the better equipped, the more prepared for war, the sooner may we hope to safeguard peace or to carry out an unavoidable war with honor and success."[26] Upton furthered this thought by warning, "So long as Congress, in time of peace, shall neglect to provide for national defense, great confusion must ensue at the beginning of our wars."[27]

---

[23] Helmuth Graf Von Moltke, *Moltke on the Art of War: Selected Writings,* trans. Daniel Hughes and Harry Bell, ed. Daniel Hughes (New York: Ballantine Books), 22.
[24] Emory Upton, *Military Policy of the US*, IX.
[25] Moltke, *Moltke on the Art of War,* 30.
[26] Moltke, *Moltke on the Art of War,* 35.
[27] Upton, *Military Policy of the US*, 92.

Upton's arguments would be sustained and repeated following WWI. The Secretary of War, in his 1921 annual report addressed the problems of being unprepared, repeating Upton's primary concern, stated,

> The present period, marking a transition from the high efficiency which we achieved during the World War at the cost of a *great initial waste of life and treasure as the penalty of unpreparedness*, must be characterized as one of the most important in our history by virtue of the duty which it imposes upon us of insuring that the lessons of the Great War are not lost, but that they are perpetuated in enduring forms of organization and continuing policy.[28] (emphasis added)

While Upton focused on the shortcomings of the military policies, Bernard Brodie addressed the results. Brodie, a key strategist and writer during the Cold War, wrote a chapter entitled "Strategy Wears a Dollar Sign" in his book *Strategy in the Missile Age*.[29] In the chapter, he challenged Upton's assertion by referring to it as the "legend that we Americans have always entered our wars unprepared."[30] He went on to state the United States won each war, that the "war against Mexico in 1846-1847 and against Spain in 1898 we won quite handily."[31] He accepted that America never "got an American-designed airplane to the front in World War I," but counters the argument by further stating, "we got plenty of other American commodities there as well as men."[32] He pointed to the United States' strategic geographic location when he stated, "we paid very little in peacetime for our security, but that is simply because we were not obliged to pay more…we were able to buy well-nigh absolute security from foreign aggression against our continental shores."[33]

Both Upton and Brodie have well founded arguments. On the one hand, the nation did suffer through numerous extended wars, which the nation could have either avoided or shortened if Congress had maintained a strong, standing army. The country would have had to bear the costs of maintaining the larger force structure, but would had avoided the costs of an extended war. Taking up Brodie's argument, the nation spent

---

[28] Department of War, *Report of the Secretary of War to the President, 1921*, 7.
[29] Brodie, *Strategy in the Missile Age* (Princeton, NJ: Princeton University Press, 1959), 358.
[30] Brodie, *Strategy in the Missile Age*, 358.
[31] Brodie, *Strategy in the Missile Age*, 358.
[32] Brodie, *Strategy in the Missile Age*, 358.
[33] Brodie, *Strategy in the Missile Age,* 359.

what was required. The nation did not suffer any grievous defeats. He agreed the nation's performance was not optimal; nevertheless, it was satisficed.

The final argument revolves around the costs of maintaining a standing military and the costs of scrambling to raise a military to fight the nation's wars. What is the right force structure, and the right funding level needed to ensure the nation's security? As discussed in chapter one, the nation cannot purchase absolute security. These debates center on the questions found at the beginning of the chapter. The following will review methods and factors to help guide the strategist in answering these questions.

Budget Methods

From this initial review of America's early history, four primary factors seem to have influenced the nation's defense budget behavior. These include the nation's cultural norm of distrusting standing armies, its geostrategic location and threat matrix, its economic goals, and finally, its national strategy. These factors resonate with the most common budgeting methods. The four methods most commonly used developing budgets are historical, threat-based, economy-based, and strategy-based.

These four models are drawn primarily from the writings of Brodie and Charles Robb. These individuals hail from different disciplines. Brodie approached the issue from an academician and strategist standpoint within his book *Strategies in the Nuclear Age.* While Brodie's perspective is from academia, Robb saw the issue from the eyes of a US Senator. He wrote an article entitled "Rebuilding a Consensus on Defense" for the Army's journal *Parameters* Winter 1996/97 edition.[34] Although he wrote the article in response to the floundering efforts to develop a realistic defense budget following the demise of the Soviet Union, the article provides a good summary of the four budgeting frameworks. The next several pages summarize each method.

Historical-Based Model

---

[34] Senator Charles Robb, "Rebuilding a Consensus on Defense," *Parameters* (Winter 1996-97), http://carlise.army mil/USAWC/parameters/96winter/robb htm. Charles Robb served in the Senate from 1988 until 2001. In the Senate, he served on the SASC, Foreign Relations and Intelligence Committees. Prior to the Senate, Senator Robb served as the Governor of Virginia and served 34 years in the Marine Corps and is a Vietnam Veteran.

The historical model has two aspects with one being the linkage to the influence of the nation's cultural norms on the defense budget and the second linked to using previous budget levels to determine future budgets within the same era. After reviewing the first part of this chapter, one can trace the cultural norms within the United States of distrusting standing armies, an aversion of foreign alliances, and avoidance of national debt or financial conservatism. These three elements drove the nation to maintain a small, relatively weak military. Once the nation's culture set the defense budget baseline, it then could become the basis for future annual budgets. Without a national event to spur additional funding, the defense budget developed its own momentum, sustaining itself. Congress, the defense structure, and the nation developed habits based on the annual peacetime budget amount apportioned to defense.

The idea of formulating budgets based on the past has links to the nation's cultural norm of distrusting standing armies. Following the end of conflicts, the nation reverts to historical budgets and force levels. The nation's culture, centered on the nation's distrust for a standing army and reliance on militias, directly influenced force structure and funding levels. Throughout the Revolutionary War, Washington had to fight this cultural norm of relying on militias rather than professional armies. The following selection, from one of the many letters Washington sent Congress, captures his frustration.

> The jealousy of a standing army, and the evils to be apprehended from, are remote…but the consequence of wanting one, according to my ideas formed from the present view of things, is certain and inevitable ruin…[t]he best criterion to work by, so fully, clearly, and decisively reprobates the practice of trusting to militia, that no man who regards order, regularity, and economy, or who has any regard for his own honor, character, or peace of mind, will risk them upon this issue.[35]

Following the Revolutionary War, Congress demonstrated this continuing distrust by disbanding the standing army on the basis that "standing armies in time of peace are inconsistent with the principles of republican government."[36] The nation would rely on the militia to secure the frontier while charging the few remaining professional soldiers with protecting the storehouses at Fort Pitt and West Point.[37] This cultural norm was evident after each conflict and even echoed in the Secretary of War's 1921 annual report

---

[35] Upton, *Military Policy of the US,* 16.
[36] Upton, *Military Policy of the US,* 16.
[37] Upton, *Military Policy of the US,* 69.

to Congress already annotated above. He stated, "permanent military policy commensurate with their great potential requirements for national defense, and yet thoroughly consistent with *their national traditions*."[38] (emphasis added) In writing "their national traditions," he is referring to the nation's norm of maintaining a small army.

Culture serves as a driving force in defining strategy, processes, and decisions. The role of culture helps explain why the United States, during its early history, drastically reduced funding for the defense structure at the end of each conflict. In his book *Modern Strategy,* Gray focused on the influence of culture on strategy and stated it is a central theme within his book.[39] He states the strategist cannot disconnect her decision process from her cultural background. As Gray observed, "[a]ll strategic behavior is cultural behavior."[40] In times of stress and disorder, the nation reverts to cultural behavior and this behavior was to reduce drastically defense funding and force structure at the end of conflicts. However, culture does not fully explain the basis for the historical model; simplicity, understandability, and reliability also play their respective part.

Being "the most common framework" for Robb, the historical budget method compares current and past budgets in "absolute and relative terms."[41] The method uses past budgets as the prime basis for the new budget. The strategist takes the preceding budget, adjusts for inflation, and produces the new budget. Without a change in environmental factors, such as new threats, a reasonable analyst would assume the same budget level allocated the previous year would be adequate for the future. While the nation enjoys relative peace, this budgeting method seems reliable and adequate.

A strategist can identify this method in use quite easily. Using this method, individuals will justify increases or decreases in defense budgets using comparisons. For example, someone supporting a strong defense might use the argument that the future budget is some percentage less in constant dollars than the past budget. His argument will be that the nation is reducing its defensive purchasing power, thereby weakening its

---

[38] Department of War, *Report of the Secretary of War to the President, 1921,* 8.
[39] Colin S. Gray, *Modern Strategy* (Oxford, England: Oxford University Press, 1999), 129.
[40] Gray, *Modern Strategy*, 129.
[41] Robb, "Rebuilding a Consensus on Defense," 6.

ability to secure the nation. In the same manner, supporters and detractors might compare defense budgets between eras. Comparing the defense budget during the height of the Cold War to the budget of the mid-1990s would show that, in real terms, the administration had curtailed the budget by only twenty percent.[42] This argument infers that additional savings within the defense budget were available due to the relative decreases in threats.

The historical method does provide consistency within the defense structure. Programs such as research and development, procurement and force structure remain stable. Programmers and planners can build programs with greater, although not complete, assurance the money will be available and grow to counter inflation. With greater assurance that funding will be available long-term, the military industry is better able to make long-term plans and thereby offer lower costs. There is less fear of sudden demobilization from year to year; thereby morale among the troops remains stronger. However, these benefits serve the organizations and individuals within the defense complex and not the nation's strategy nor does it guarantee national security.

Reliance upon this model can produce a gap between the real purpose of budgets (purchasing the means to accomplish the national strategy), and the organization's goal (survival measured by budget levels) develops. Gray also adds to this argument cautioning the nation not to establish budget levels to support the organization when he stated, "armed forces exist primarily to serve as a more or less complex instrument of the grand strategy of the state; they are *not funded to function as a well-oiled machine that is an end in itself.* The benefits do not always serve the national security objectives. Military power, therefore, should be balanced against best estimates of the country's need for it."[43] (emphasis added) As Robb stated, the "framework is good for rhetoric, but too simplistic for real world planning."[44] He added, "we're not spending enough now because we spent more in the past is hardly a sound basis for planning."[45]

The historical method is good as a benchmark, one the strategist must considered when building budgets, but it should not be the primary influence. While useful as a

---

[42] Robb, "Rebuilding a Consensus on Defense," 6.
[43] Colin S. Gray, *Explorations in Strategy* (Westport, CT: Praeger, 1996), 21.
[44] Robb, "Rebuilding a Consensus on Defense," 6.
[45] Robb, "Rebuilding a Consensus on Defense," 6.

starting point, the historical method must be linked to threats or changing geopolitical objectives.

Threat-Based Method

Two factors drive the threat-based method: intentions and capabilities. The interplay of these two factors defines the seriousness or level of the threats faced by a nation. The threat posed by a readily identified hostile, but capabilities poor enemy, might be deemed by the nation as a low threat, or possibly, a growing threat. In contrast, an enemy with uncertain intentions, but with vast capabilities might serve as the basis for building up the nation's defense. Measuring the capabilities of another nation's military should be relatively objective; the key is access to information and intelligence. Within this calculus, it can be challenging to determine an opponent's intentions. The evaluation of intentions is more subjective and prone to be divined more from the strategist's perceptions. Normally, it is the threat-based method that justifies the opening of the nation's purse strings for defense spending.

The military policies and defense funding of early America had ties to a threat-based methodology. While the historical method is inward looking, the threat-based method is more externally oriented and there is a natural tension between the two methods. The nation's optimal choice was to rely solely on the militia to address external threats. Congress disbanded the standing army shortly after the end of the Revolutionary War, and the nation made the conscious decision not to fund or support a navy. While the nation's culture and economy influenced these decisions, it was external threats that spurred the nation to change its policy, and fund a standing army and navy. The nation would reestablish the professional army due to threats from Indians and domestic insecurity, while Congress would fund the building of naval ships and a navy due to confirmed threats on the high seas. Threats acted as a counter to the nation's cultural norm and economic concerns. However, the threats had to exceed another obstacle to overcome further Congressional reservations.

That obstacle was the nation's geostrategic location. The nation's geographic location provided another environmental factor that allowed the nation to maintain a small standing army and rely on the militia. Prior to aircraft, intercontinental missiles, or weapons of mass destruction (WMD) carried by small groups, the United States had the time needed to react to threats. The geographic location of the nation allowed for the time and space to respond; threats to national security were distant. Threats from the east would have to traverse oceans to strike the continental United States. European nations did not have the capabilities to transport large armies across the Atlantic, invade the nation, and threaten its sovereignty.

The ocean would serve as a barrier to any serious threats throughout America's early history. The Secretary of War, in his 1890 annual report echoed the justification for a small army based on the barrier when he wrote, "We are separated by an ocean from the powers which maintain great armies…no hostile force is likely to seek an encounter with us on our own soil. We have, therefore, little to fear from invasion, and are free from the necessity of maintaining large standing armies or of fortifying against land attacks."[46] While the ocean provided a barrier against European aggression, the nation did address threats along its western frontier.

The threat posed by American Indians on the frontiers and domestic unrest initially justified a standing army. Congress recognized the Indian threat as a nuisance restricting westward expansion; and could not tolerate internal domestic unrest. The view that the nation could rely on militia changed as the nation suffered defeats. Between the Revolutionary War and the War of 1812, the number and scope of the threats motivated Congress to increase the size of the professional military. Shay's Rebellion, Harmar's Miami expedition against the Indians in Florida, St. Clair's defeat by the Indians, and the Whiskey Rebellion in Pennsylvania refocused Congress' attention; the militia could not address these conflicts in a timely and effective manner. As a result, Congress increased the army to 800, and latter to 5,000, and provided the President with powers to increase the army's size in the event of an invasion. [47]

Threats, such as Indian or domestic turmoil, exist across a spectrum. As can be surmised from the discussion above, not every threat is the same. Brodie, within his writings, broke the idea of threats into two useful concepts, the "opponent's intentions versus his capabilities."[48] It is important to understand these two threat characteristics.

---

[46] Department of War, *Report of the Secretary of War for the Year, 1890* (Washington DC: Government Printing Office, 1891), 5.
[47] Upton, *Military Policy of the US,* 69-72.
[48] Brodie, *Strategy in the Missile Age,* 377.

The region's strongest army might border the nation, and this fact might or might not represent a threat. The question the strategist has to ask is "what are the intentions of that border nation?" England, with the world's strongest navy, bordered the United States via the ocean; yet, the United States consciously decided, initially, not to fund or maintain a navy. The threats posed by England did not suffice to justify increasing the nation's military, thereby incurring debt.

The threat-based method seems optimal when the nation is faced with a hostile nation with great capabilities. When Brodie was writing his book, the United States had a readily defined opponent in the Soviet Union. The Soviet Union had the capabilities and intentions to spread communism around the world. Having an enemy like the Soviet Union would seem to make this method easier and the nation would simply acquire capabilities necessary to gain a continuous advantage over the enemy by measuring the relative sizes of navies, land, and air forces thereby allowing the nation to identify gaps and budget to fill them. With this method, the nation can readily determine the level of funding needed to counter the enemy. The "missile gap" of the late 1950s is an example of this argument. However, like the missile gap episode, threat-based approaches can distort the true strategic outlook.

On the other hand, how does a nation use the threat-based model when there are no identifiable opponents? Robb wrote his article when the nation lacked a distinct peer opponent. Defense budget critics pointed to the fact the United States was no longer facing the Warsaw Pact, but the defense budget had only decreased by 20 percent.[49] The nation's defense budget was greater than the eight closest potential opponents' defense budgets combined. Defense budget supporters defended the budget based on the nation's relative strength against the world, not against any one possible opponent. This was the era when the two major theater construct first entered the National Security Strategy.[50] Advocates stated the United States required a large defense budget to maintain the capability to fight two distinct campaigns such as against Iraq and North Korea. Members of this group also cautioned against a rising China and a resurgent Russia; these defense advocates used capability-based arguments to sustain defense funding.

---

[49] Robb, "Rebuilding a Consensus on Defense," 2.
[50] Robb, "Rebuilding a Consensus on Defense," 3.

The discussion so far has focused on the capabilities aspect of potential enemies and not on their respective intentions. Thomas Schelling, in his book *Arms and Influence*, stated, "It is a tradition in military planning to attend to an enemy's capabilities, not his intentions."[51] However, he further stated and warned, "deterrence is about intentions" and should be the strategist's focus, for deterrence is linked to political objectives. [52] He goes as far as to state that the strategist is "not just estimating enemy intentions but influencing them."[53] In Gray's third meaning of balanced forces, he also addressed the idea that capabilities must be "balanced against the calculated demands." [54]

What are the intentions of our potential enemy? This is a difficult question to answer. In Brodie's writings, he addressed the difficulty, writing, "foreign intentions provide us cues for our defense efforts only when they are clear-cut and either conspicuously friendly or plainly warlike."[55] As stated in chapter one, defense budgets and strategies are easier to develop in times of certainty. When the nation is at war, the threat is clear and the nation spends what is necessary to secure political objectives. Brodie further stated, "The margin of possible error is usually greater in reading the opponent's intentions than in reading their military capabilities."[56] Attempting to understand the intentions and psychology of the opponent is at best problematic.

Robert Jervis, a professor of Political Science, wrote one of the masterpieces of international relations when he penned *Perception and Misperception in International Politics*. Published in 1976, Jervis' book covered a wide range of issues and ideas within the book regarding how nations, in particular individuals, process external stimuli and form perceptions. A number of these concepts have direct linkage to our discussion of tying budgets to threats and intentions. To understand the opponent's intentions, the strategist must make assumptions and inferences. The opponents of the United States are not likely to publish a national security document listing objectives or describing actions. Therefore, the strategist will need to study the opponent and develop a useful analysis.

---

[51] Thomas C. Schelling, *Arms and Influence* (London: Yale University Press, 1966), 35.
[52] Schelling, *Arms and Influence,* 35.
[53] Schelling, *Arms and Influence,* 35.
[54] Gray, *Explorations in Strategy*, 21.
[55] Brodie, *Strategy in the Missile Age*, 378.
[56] Brodie, *Strategy in the Missile Age*, 378.

There are obstacles in this process to include the tendency for humans to assimilate information with pre-existing beliefs. Strategists might fall to the error of mirror imaging, therefore characterizing the opponent's actions in his own terms.[57] Within this problem, the strategist views the opponent's actions, no matter how innocent, as threats. This creates cognitive distortions of the opponent's real intentions.[58] The normal human reaction to cognitive dissonance takes two paths. Jervis stated, "The existence of dissonance…will motivate the person to try to reduce dissonance and achieve consonance." And "the person will actively avoid situations and information which would likely increase the dissonance."[59] Within this construct, basing budgets on threats (opponent's intentions) is fraught with errors. It is difficult to gain a clear understanding of the opponent's intentions.

A second concept from Jervis addresses the capabilities side of the argument. This relates to the spiral theory. When a strategist characterizes the opponent's actions as threats, the strategist will justify increasing the budget for weapons to counter the threat; the strategist must maintain an advantage. If both opponents follow this path, then each will respond to the other's action by increasing their power to maintain balance or an advantage.[60] Each will attempt to build or purchase the stronger weapon in reaction to the other's respective behavior. Brodie connected the spiral theory to budgeting when he states, "It is true and important that increases in our defense budget will probably have certain effects upon Soviet behavior, particularly with respect to their own defense budget."[61] Following this path leads to a weapons and budgeting race.

There are, however, a number of problems with the threat-based approach. Whether the strategist takes a capabilities, intentions or mixed approach, she experiences uncertainty. When there is an opponent, there is an uncertainty regarding the opponent's intentions. There is also uncertainty and complexity when there is not a readily identifiable enemy. The nation can focus in the wrong direction and fail to detect new

---

[57] Robert Jervis, *Perception and Misperception in International Politics* (Princeton, NJ: Princeton University Press, 1976), 353-355. Jervis lists multiple problems with nation's attempting to determine opponent identities along with their intentions, how an individual's predisposed beliefs, experiences, and international knowledge colors one's beliefs and cognitive understanding leading to misperceptions.
[58] Jervis, *Perception and Misperception,* 130.
[59] Jervis, *Perception and Misperception,* 382.
[60] Jervis, *Perception and Misperception,* 62.
[61] Brodie, *Strategy in the Missile Age,* 379.

threats or capabilities. As Robb pointed out, the method "overemphasizes immediate and obvious threats while underrating future unknowns."[62] While the ability to identify an enemy and the enemy's intentions is problematic, when the threat-based method is used alone, it becomes the sole basis for the budget. The process can spiral out of control, bankrupting the nation the strategist is attempting to secure.

A threat-based approach to formulate budgets does have benefits. As long as it is not the sole means, the method can help the strategist determine what means to fund to counter possible threats. It helps the nation balance the armed forces for Gray's fourth meaning of balanced forces, a "tolerable fit with unique national strategic preferences and needs, as well as to exploit national strengths and provide suitable cover for national weaknesses."[63] Understanding the threat environment, capabilities and intentions, is essential to develop national strategies in accomplishing geopolitical objectives. The strategist must tie the threat-based argument to strategic goals and the national strategy. With this understood, the strategist can begin to frame the budget while understanding and stretching what the nation can afford.

Economy-Based Method

The manner in which one frames the economy-based funding question helps focus the process. If the question is stated, "How much is left for defense?" the emphasis is on the economy. The question implies the nation funds domestic programs first and avoids defense spending. Both the Truman and Eisenhower administration took this approach, with each administration believing in balancing the budget, eliminating debt, funding domestic programs, and applying the remaining tax revenue to defense funding. The courses of action or strategies available become the lowest cost options with the strategist having to allocate limited funding and purchasing the means most likely to accomplish the nation's geopolitical goals. On the other hand, the defense program has greater importance when the question is framed, "How much can the nation afford for defense?" This method implies allowance for deficits and debt. The nation's security outweighs the risk of incurring budget deficits and running up the national debt. There is a more nuance

---

[62] Robb, "Rebuilding a Consensus on Defense," 7.
[63] Gray, *Explorations in Strategy*, 21.

attempt to allocate funds with the administration determining the marginal utility of that next federal dollar. The nation must determine if there is greater utility applying the last dollar to the defense budget or domestic programs; the problem becomes more an economy of effort debate. While security is a valued commodity, absolute security is not possible or affordable in an uncertain and complex world.

The problem of national security does not have an end state or final solution. Remember, the strategist must achieve a continuous advantage to help ensure security or achieve political milestones, not a political end-state. Given this condition, the nation must maintain and strengthen the economy constantly. The nation needs to support policies to sustain the economy, thereby maintaining the ability to support its security. Brodie stated, "It is obviously true that national military security over the long term requires a healthy economy, for the economy must carry the burden."[64] The strategist must also remember Gray's caution that "inadequate defense expenditure assuredly will imperil the physical security of the country, as well as the health of the economy"[65] when addressing the balance. It is a struggle to strike the right balance both in the short and long term.

Brodie does provide a useful method to evaluate the relative health of the economy. The administration can use the method to determine if its spending policies are harming or sustaining the economy. Brodie's method includes the following metrics: reasonable proportion of gross national product (GNP) reinvested in capital expenditures, a growing standard of living, inflation kept under control, and low unemployment.[66] One might notice that Brodie does not include national debt is in his metrics. Brodie addressed debt and did not find it problematic for the nation. Influenced by a leading economist of the 1950s, he stated national debt was acceptable because the Americans held the debt. External debt, on the other hand, was to be avoided. At the time, the United States was a net creditor in the world.[67] The debate regarding national debt is ongoing today; but there is a critical limit the nation should not exceed.

---

[64] Brodie, *Strategy in the Missile Age*, 367.
[65] Gray, *Explorations in Strategy,* 115.
[66] Brodie, *Strategy in the Missile Age*, 367.
[67] Brodie, *Strategy in the Missile Age*, 368.

There is another on-going discussion regarding the relationship between defense spending and the economy. In the past, many assumed the relationship was a trade-off between guns and butter, "and that military spending had to occur at the expense of other sectors of the economy."[68] Many, though, believe there is a positive relationship between the two, enough of a positive relationship that defense spending should be tied to the nation's GNP. For example, Brodie linked the decline in defense budgets during the mid-1950s with the "relative stagnation of the economy" in discussing the relationship between defense budgets and GNP. He questions whether there is something "sacred" about keeping the defense budget below 10 percent of the national GNP.[69] Many associate the increased spending associated with World War II as the stimulant that pulled the United States out of the Great Depression.[70] John Maynard Keynes' ideas of government spending and economic growth became a justification of large military budgets. A number of scholars claimed those advocating large defense budgets based on Keynesian concept had bastardized as his work into "military Keynesianism,"[71] The "virtuous circle of mutually reinforcing military spending and economic growth" was so strong that Harvard economist Sumner Slichter explained, "that as long as Cold War spending persisted a severe economic depression was difficult to conceive."[72]

Martin Feldstein, another Harvard economist, argued for the positive relationship between defense spending and the economy as recently as January of 2009. He addressed the House Democratic Steering and Policy Committee regarding the pending economic stimulus bill. Within his prepared statement, Feldstein addressed the overarching problems of the economy, and how the stimulus package would fill the gap, while newly implemented policies corrected past problems. During his comments, he addressed his surprise that the current stimulus bill did not allocate funding to defense and was discouraged to read that the incoming Obama administration would reduce

---

[68] John B. Foster, Hannah Holleman, and Robert W. McChesney, "The U.S. Imperial Triangle and Military Spending" *Monthly Review,* Oct 2008, 2.
[69] Brodie, *Strategy in the Missile Age*, 371.
[70] Foster, "U.S. Imperial Triangle," 3.
[71] Foster, "U.S. Imperial Triangle," 3.
[72] Foster, "U.S. Imperial Triangle," 5.

defense spending over the next few years. Feldstein held that increasing the force structure and purchasing equipment would be healthy for the economy.[73]

These arguments overshadow the reasons for defense spending. While the nation's treasure is limited, and the strategist must balance the national security and economic health of the nation, these concerns must remain as constraints in building a strategy based on political objectives. The nation will spend what is necessary during a war; the consequences of spending less are not acceptable. It is during relatively peaceful eras that the budgeting problem becomes more acute. Linking defense budget to a percentage of GNP or allocating what is left after domestic programs are funded is too simplistic; the methods are devoid of serious thinking that can ensure the security of the nation. Again, the nation and strategist must strike the right balance between the economy and the nation's security.

Strategy-Based Model

The strategist, in determining the amount of funding for defense, must use each of the three previous methods. To develop a national security strategy, the strategist must understand the nation's culture, recognize the nation's potential threats, and spend within imposed economic constraints. A strategy, as defined in chapter one, is the linkage between means and political ends; it is Gray's bridge. The budget determines what means the nation can obtain. However, the strategist needs some beacon or guidance to determine what means are needed.

The nation's geopolitical goals should be the strategist's beacon. Historical expenditures, the nation capabilities and intentions, as well as its opponent's capabilities and intentions, and economic factors should serve as guideposts or limits. For each dollar spent, there should be some relative marginal utility justifying the expenditure.[74] The various means purchased must be linked to a national security objective to calculate that utility. As Brodie frames the issue, the process should be, "the most efficient utilization of potential and available resources to the end of enhancing our security."[75] The

---

[73] Martin Feldstein, *The Economic Stimulus and Sustained Economic Growth*, Full Statement for the House Democratic Steering and Policy Committee, 7 January 2009, 11-12.
[74] Brodie, *Strategy in the Missile Age*, 380-382.
[75] Brodie, *Strategy in the Missile Age*, 378.

administration must spread the budget allocation to ensure a balanced force that the nation can use to counter different sets of "possible or probable circumstances."[76] The strategist should use the concept of marginal utility to spread each additional dollar. To accomplish this, the process requires in-depth analysis, not some simplified method linking the budget to a subjective percentage of the nation's GNP, what is left in the treasury or an amount equivalent to that spent the year prior.

The nation's original strategy of avoiding foreign entanglements and using its geographic location to deter foreign threats helped justify a small military force and navy. Whether this strategy was developed before or after considering the threat and economic environment is not as relevant as ensuring that future military and security policies consider them. Each administration must examine the geopolitical environment, especially following the end of a conflict, to establish a strategy that will allow for Dolman's continuous advantage. Within that environment, the strategist must examine and measure the threats posed by external actors, understand the nation's economy and ability to raise revenue, and take advantage of the nation's inherent attributes such as geographic location and resources. Based on this detailed review and analysis, the strategist or political leaders can develop a long-term strategy linked to geopolitical objectives.

The nation's geopolitical objectives then serve as milestones as the nation determines the allocation of funding between defense and domestic programs, how to tax and generate revenue, and use the various instruments of power. Instead of the defense budget being solely justified due to external threats, what is left of the budget or by historical practices, it is tied to missions supporting national security strategy. When the budget is tied to a strategy, one accepted and endorsed by political leaders and supported by the populace, the nation should be willing to endure the costs and appropriate the needed funding. Again, this linkage is very apparent in times of war, when the nation supports the conflict. It is during times of relative peace that this process becomes more complicated and the process requires greater analysis and review to ensure any errors are marginalized.

---

[76] Brodie, *Strategy in the Missile Age*, 379.

Conclusion

Budgeting for the nation's security is an economy of force problem at the grand strategic level. While getting the principle right at the operational level can be the difference between a battle victory and loss; failure to balance resources and properly budget limited resources at the grand strategic level can result in the loss of freedom. The strategist's decisions today have lasting impact, determining the means decades into the future. Gray stated, "the problem is to know what to buy, when, and in what quantities, far ahead of the validation of the need by events."[77] The strategist, in Gray's opinion, has to be an alchemist to get the mix right. He must be a fortuneteller and an experienced guide while venturing across the "fairly hostile jungle" of the budget process.[78]

Even when a nation has taken due caution to fund national security, the nation often finds it has fallen short under the test that is war. Reading the literature, one finds a number of authors ringing the warning bell. Robb stated, "History has shown repeatedly that the next major threat can be difficult to predict."[79] Gray quoted from Field Marshal Sir Nigel Bagnall when writing "over the centuries identifying a nation's future strategic priorities has proved to be a very imprecise art, and as a result peacetime force structures have seldom proved relevant when put to the test of war."[80] Funding a nation's defense has always been problematic; the nation cannot purchase absolute security. General Rupert Smith's quote at the beginning of this chapter repeats this claim. All agree the perfect strategy and funding decisions are not possible within a complex and uncertain world. However, the strategist cannot throw in the towel. The strategist, "instead, has the charge…to search for a strategy and force structure 'right enough' that should be tolerant of inevitable errors."[81] In other words, the strategist needs to ensure the errors are survivable; the nation has the time and space to adjust.

There are several problems inherent in formulating a defense budget absent linkages to strategic objectives. Although a good starting point, the historical basis is

---

[77] Gray, *Explorations in Strategy*, 113.
[78] Colin S. Gray, *Fighting Talk, Forty Maxims on War, Peace and Strategy* (Westport, CT: Praeger Security International, 2007), 138.
[79] Robb, "Rebuilding a Consensus on Defense," 7.
[80] Gray, *Explorations in Strategy*, 23.
[81] Gray, *Explorations in Strategy*, 112.

disconnected from emerging threats and a changing geopolitical environment. Arguments promoting increases or decreases in defense spending are simplistic and the respective advocates base their logic on the budget's relations to past budgets. Proponents fail to address security objectives and the security environment. While the threat-based method does address the security environment, the method can be problematic. A strategist, attempting to justify budgets based on opponent capabilities, is prone to engaging in a competition to build the most powerful weapons, and this competition then drives the budget. Attempting to determine the opponent's intentions, as shown, is difficult. Traps include mirror imaging and attempts to resolve cognitive dissonance that color the opponents' actions by prior perceived beliefs. The threat-based method also focuses the strategist attention to the more obvious threats, thereby blinding him to new and emergent threats. On the economic score, Robb further stated the threat-based method "underestimates the importance of economic security and the value of security-enhancing actions less directly tied to the threats."[82] Robb argued that the nation must not jeopardize the nation's economy by overspending on defense requirements. While surely a restraint to the overall budget, the economy-based argument can be fraught with challenges. The nation cannot link the defense budget to a certain percentage of GDP or limit the budget to what remains after funding domestic priorities. This process is simplistic and does not guarantee security; the decisions must be tied to an overarching strategy. The strategist must heed Gray's warning that spending too little to protect the economy risks the nation.[83] The strategist must analyze the marginal utility of each dollar spent with a goal of balancing the military force and economy. Moreover, he must do this within the context of the nation's geopolitical objectives.

The United States, rooted in the cultural baggage of distrusting a standing army, enjoying a relatively secure geostrategic location, and practicing fiscal conservatism, adopted military funding policies that were guardian in nature.[84] Congress established the initial Continental Army of 800 to counter the threat of American Indians along the

---

[82] Robb, "Rebuilding a Consensus on Defense," 7.

[83] Gray, *Explorations in Strategy*, 115.

[84] Brian M. Linn, *The Echo of Battle: The Army's Way of War* (Cambridge, MA: Harvard University Press, 2007), 5. Linn, within his book describes three martial philosophies including the hero, manager and the guardian. The guardians saw the primary threat to the nation from sudden attack along the coast line and supported building coastal defenses; it relied on the oceans, distrust of alliances and the coastal defenses minimized need for large standing armies.

western frontier and believed the threat of a European invasion was low. When the British and French began to board American merchant vessels on the high seas, Congress recognized the threat to American commerce. Congress responded by allocating funding for the construction of seven naval vessels thereby creating the Navy. It was these threat, both capabilities and intentions, which drove the nation to provide more funding for defense. While these threats opened up the nation's purse, the nation's strategy of avoiding foreign entanglements, its geographic location, difficulty in balancing the budget due to limited revenue streams, and reluctance to raise taxes pulled the strings tight. Throughout America's early history, the threat of war was the prime reason the nation opened the purse and paid for a larger military force. The other budgeting models provide the reasons why, as soon as the war was over, the nation, led by Congress, cut funding and force levels.

These same dynamics were evident as the nation, led by President Truman, concluded World War II as the victors and as the most powerful nation on earth. With the Axis threats eliminated, concern with the nation's economy would reinforce the nation's tendency to demobilize and cut defense spending. The nation's Wilsonian strategy promoting world peace followed by a containment policy relied heavily on a strong economy rather than a strong military. The economy, along with geopolitical goals, trumped the threat of an expanding Soviet Union.

Chapter 3

THE ECONOMY TRUMPS DEFENSE BUDGETS

As World War II concluded in 1945, President Truman, within his first few weeks in office, began the process of demobilizing the military and cutting the defense budget. Within just eighteen months, the administration cut the military and its funding by 90 percent. This should not have surprised anyone; Truman was just repeating the country's habit of cutting force levels and budgets at the end of the nation's conflicts. As demonstrated in the previous chapter, the United States adopted and had maintained a cultural norm during its first 150 years of mistrusting standing armies, attempting to avoid and eliminate national debt, and avoiding foreign entanglements. While the historical model, reflected in this cultural norm, provides some explanation addressing why the nation cut defense funding and force structure, it does not explain why the Truman Administration made these cuts in light of the growing communist threat.

By reviewing Truman's defense budget decisions using the budget models reviewed in the previous chapter, a greater understanding can be obtained of the tensions that pulled on the nation's purse strings. The economy-based model best explains Truman's driving desire to balance the nation's budget to cut the nation's debt and strengthen the nation's economy. With a strong economy converted back to domestic production, Truman could support the recovery of Western Europe; this objective was a key leg to the nation's strategy of blocking and containing communism. Truman envisioned a Wilsonian world providing a better peace than that experienced following the end of World War I. Within this strategic outlook, the world needed global economic reforms promoting free trade, democratic forms of government and an international organization providing oversight. While these factors, along with the nation's historical norm, pulled the defense purse strings close, the threats, in both capabilities and intentions, presented by the Soviet Union attempted to pry that same purse open.

This chapter's purpose is to study the Truman administration's decision process. In particular, the chapter will examine how the factors influenced Truman's defense funding decisions. This case study examines the following questions. What were the threats, the economic conditions, and means available to the Truman administration?

How did Truman develop his security strategy? Lastly, what budgeting methodology dominated the decision process?

This case study, as well as the following case, is being conducted from a macro perspective. In particular, it is reviewing defense budget decisions from the perspective of Presidents Truman and Bush. Additionally, in analyzing the decisions, the models are being used to provide a perspective that simply adds context to the decision process. The case studies do not address the influences of Congress, bureaucracies, and other pertinent factors in any detail. As such, the reader should not construe these case studies and the findings as the sole reasons for the respective administration's decisions.

Setting the Stage

The allies had all but won World War II when Truman became president. By that time, the "Big Three" had already drafted the design for the new world order. The two conferences held at Teheran in November 1943 and Yalta in February 1945 had focused on redrawing borders and creating an international governing body, as well as determining the fate of the Axis powers. John Lewis Gaddis, in his recently written book *The Cold War: A New History*, stated, "The leaders of the victorious Grand Alliance…had already exchanged their own handshakes, toasts, and hopes for a better world at two wartime summits."[1] The allies seemed to be in accord and working toward that better world. While the alliance was strong when the outcome of the war was in jeopardy, this relatively harmonious relationship began to unravel as the outcome increasingly favored the allies.

As the war concluded and the allies met in conference to plan the post-war world, each of the allies positioned itself to secure its respective geopolitical objectives. The leaders discussed two types of issues at their conferences. The first centered on near term objectives, which included their affirmation for the unconditional surrender of Germany, setting the invasion date for France, and setting the conditions for the Soviet Union to declare war on Japan. There was disagreement regarding dates and the efforts being demonstrated, but there was consensus on the ultimate objective of unconditional surrender. The second grouping consisted of post-war issues; among these-issues certain

---

[1] John Lewis Gaddis, *The Cold War: A New History* (London, England: Penguin Press, 2005), 5-6.

ones, such as creation of the United Nations, setting the borders and elections for Poland, and occupation policy and the final disposition of Germany were more contentious, and these disagreements foreshadowed the coming Cold War. [2]

Truman was not fully aware of the political agreements between the "Big Three" at the conferences or the many disagreements arising between Stalin and the rest of the allies. Although Truman supported most of President Roosevelt's programs, Roosevelt had kept him in the dark regarding several foreign policy issues while Truman focused on spearheading Roosevelt's domestic political agenda on Capitol Hill. This ignorance included the Manhattan Project; a program he would not be aware of until his first full day as president.[3] Truman faced multiple challenges assuming the power of the presidency and he would spend his first few weeks getting up to speed on the issues. It was against this background that Truman assumed command.

As he navigated through this geopolitical landscape and a world economy ravaged and transformed by war, his administration would oversee a program drastically reducing the force structure and defense budget. Truman inherited an Army of over eight million soldiers and a budget exceeding $74 billion. By 1947, that same Army was sized at just 898 thousand and a budget of just seven billion dollars.[4] This reflected a tenfold decrease in both force size in budget. (The Navy and Air Force experienced similar cuts)[5] These cuts were conducted at the same time the Army was occupying Japan and Germany, and the actions or inactions of the Soviets foreshadowed the coming Cold War. How does one explain these funding and force cuts within the described geopolitical environment? The following four budgeting models provide explanations.

Historical-Based Model

The nation's historical behavior did factor in the administration's drive to reduce the defense budget and defensive force structure. The cultural norms of maintaining a small defense force, the nation's desires to rely on a militia, and avoidance of debt do help explain the cuts to the military force and defense budgets. The nation could and

[2] Gaddis, *The Cold War*, 5-6.
[3] Truman, *Memoirs*, 10.
[4] United States Department of Defense, *National Defense Estimates for FY2009* (Washington: Department of Defense, 2008), *67*
[5] United States Department of Defense, *National Defense Estimates for FY2009*, 67.

would not maintain a Spartan-like nation totally focused on its military force and power; it would not sustain the force levels achieved during World War II. While Truman wanted to eliminate the draft, thereby cutting the force levels and budget even more, he was constrained by the requirement for occupation forces in Japan and Germany. Even with this constraint, Truman would quickly begin cutting the defense budget, take steps to convert the nation to a domestic focused industry, and reduce defensive force levels below military recommended levels, all in an effort to balance the budget.

World War II was very close to being a total war. America employed the majority of the nation's people and industry in the war effort and there would have to be cuts; the nation could not sustain, nor did it need, the same force structure. In addition to the impractical possibility of maintaining such a large force, American's were ready to reunite families, and military members were ready to return home and begin their lives. For the common American, the norm was to answer the call of duty when it rang; it was not the norm to remain part of the professional military force once the war was over.

Truman wanted the force level cuts to be orderly and well planned. However, for military leaders like Generals Marshall and Eisenhower, the reductions were too quick and drastic, and they resurrected Upton's earlier warnings.[6] Even against these warnings and requests, the nation continued the process. The nation's response resulted in cutting the Army's force structure nearly in half from a high of 8,266,373 in June of 1945 to 4,228,936 in December 1945.[7] This occurred over just six months. By the beginning of 1948, the Army's total strength was down to 575,314; this figure was fifty thousand less than what was on hand in December 1940.[8] This drawdown occurred while the demand for forces was increasing due to occupation requirements and growing signs of hostile Soviet intentions.

The first step in reducing the force structure was shutting down the pipeline. In August of 1945, the president started the process by reducing the number drafted per month from eighty thousand to fifty thousand. Truman stated this was required bringing

---

[6] George C. Marshall, *Biennial Reports of the Chief of Staff of the United States Army to the Secretary of War: 1 July 1939 – 30 June 1945,* (Washington, DC: Government Printing Office, 1965), 207-209.

[7] Department of Defense, *Annual Report of the Secretary of the Army, 1948,* Washington: Government Printing Office, 1948), 294 – 297.

[8] Department of Defense, *Annual Report of the Secretary of the Army, 1948,* 294 – 297.

"most of the boys home."[9] Truman sent a letter to Congress addressing the cut in draft numbers stating he wanted to stop the draft completely and bring the troops home as quickly as possible, but was constrained by the alliance due to the need for occupation duties.[10] As to the force structure needed for occupation duties, Truman did take the advice of Generals Eisenhower and MacArthur setting the occupation force size at 1.2 million.[11] Nevertheless, against the military's recommendation, Truman would even cut this force size as quickly as possible.

A second historical factor driving the drawdown was the nation's preference for a militia. Instead of increasing or maintaining the force structure to address the growing Russian threat, Truman and the Army turned to universal training. The Army, just as in the First World War, had problems with mobilization during the war's early phases. Universal training was the proposed solution by providing a reserve force that could be mobilized effectively allowing for greater, quicker force projection. The nation would train every able body American male, providing each with basic military knowledge and thereby construct a new Minuteman force, ready to answer the nation's call.[12] This option was also the low cost solution; it would help address the nation's record $269 billion debt balance.[13]

In the same vein, the nation was not used to carrying a heavy debt burden. The nation held a national debt of just $3 billion in 1916. The costs of WWI would spike the debt to $25 billion by 1920. The Roaring Twenties would see the debt drop back down to $16 billion only to double by 1939 due to the Great Depression. In World War II, the defense budget ballooned, as expected, and by 1944, national debt actually exceeded the national GDP. The war increased the nation's debt from $40 billion in 1939 to $269 billion by 1945; these were record levels of debt.[14] For a populist tied to America's

---

[9] *Public Papers of the Presidents of the United States: Harry S. Truman, 1945* (Washington, DC: Government Printing Office, 1946), 228.

[10] *Public Papers of the Presidents of the United States: Harry S. Truman, 1945*, 228.

[11] *Public Papers: Truman, 1945,* 240.

[12] Marshall, *Biennial Reports,* 210-211.

[13] United States Department of the Treasury, "National Debt Historical Charts," http://www.treasurydirect.gov/govt/reports/pd/histdebt/histdebt.htm (accessed 15 March 2009)

[14] United States Department of the Treasury, "National Debt Historical Charts," http://www.treasurydirect.gov/govt/reports/pd/histdebt/histdebt.htm (accessed 15 March 2009)

historic past, Truman could and would not support these levels of indebtedness. Truman had to ensure the nation's economy was converted and rejuvenated.

One of Truman's top priorities upon becoming president was to balance the budget. Even before the surrender of Germany, Truman announced at a press conference he expected to cut the government defense budget by seven billion dollars. Most of these savings were the result of cutting shipbuilding in the 1946 budget.[15] He informed the speaker of the house that the budget drawdown would be done in an orderly manner, and only after reflecting upon the strategic consequences; his administration would only send budget cut proposals following the conclusion of careful analysis.[16] During the month of September 1945, Truman sent over multiple budget reduction requests totaling over $39 billion, and recalled Congress back to session to address additional budget cuts and his 21-point reconversion program.[17] The reconversion program included demobilization of forces, the cancelation and settlement of war contracts, and clearing out war plants to permit peacetime production. While Truman designed the reconversion program to keep inflation in check, employment up and ensure the unemployed had a safety net, the program also set the nation on track to balance the budget and tackle the national debt.[18]

The nation's cultural norms of maintaining a small defense force, relying on a militia and reluctance at incurring excessive debt provide some explanatory power regarding the defense cuts between 1944 and 1948. As Gray observed, culture helps explain strategic behavior; the nation's cultural norms help explain the quick demobilization of forces and defense funding cuts experienced at the end of World War II as displayed in Table 2.[19] While the historical model provides some assistance in understanding the drawdown, the construct does not explain why these cuts continued as the Truman administration recognized the Soviet threat during the same period. There must be additional variables that drove Truman to continue the force reductions and budget cuts.

---

[15] *Public Papers: Truman, 1945,* 37.
[16] *Public Papers, Truman, 1945,* 102-103.
[17] *Public Papers: Truman, 1945,* 309.
[18] *Public Papers: Truman, 1945,* 309.
[19] Colin Gray, *Modern Strategy* (Oxford, England: Oxford Press, 1999), 148-151, 155.

Table 2: Post World War II Defense Budgets, Forces, and Debt

Year	Defense Budget	Force Structure	National Debt
1944	$74B	8,052,693	$201B
1945	$48B	4,228,936	$258B
1946	$40B	1,319,483	$269B
1947	$7B	898,472	$258B
1948	$6B	574,723	$253B

Complied from various sources: United States Department of Defense, *National Defense Estimates for FY2009* (Washington: Department of Defense, 2008). Department of the Army, *Annual Report of the Secretary of the Army, 1948* (Washington: Government Printing Office, 1949). United States Department of the Treasury, "National Debt Historical Charts," http://www.treasurydirect.gov/govt/reports/pd/histdebt/histdebt.htm (accessed 15 March 2009)

Strategy-Based Model

Truman was a proponent of Wilsonian principles of world peace and this would drive the formulation of his geopolitical goals. Though Truman was credited with a solid foundation in domestic issues due to his Congressional experience, general opinion, as he took the presidency, deemed him to be "untutored in world affairs."[20] Nevertheless, he held utopian views of world peace that included programs promoting greater international trade, and creation of an international political governing organization, and he fought America's tendency toward isolationism; a norm tied to the nation's historical past. Truman, as Vice-President, delivered a number of speeches aimed at warning fellow citizens that America could not "sit smugly behind a Maginot Line."[21] The world was changing and America could not sit comfortable protected by the oceans. With this as the background, Truman established a strategy with three key geopolitical objectives that would allow him to reduce the size of the nation's defense budget and force structure.

Truman's three geopolitical objectives included creating the United Nations (UN), establishing of a world policing organization and ensuring the United Kingdom could manage European stability. While these objectives were optimistic, Truman remained pragmatic with regard to the Soviets. Truman stated in 1941 that the Soviets were as

[20] Arnold A. Offner, *Another Such Victory: President Truman and the Cold War, 1945-1953* (Stanford, CA: Stanford University Press, 2002), ix.
[21] Offner, *Another Such Victory*, 19.

40

untrustworthy as "Hitler and Al Capone."[22] Nevertheless, he needed Stalin's buy-in to ensure the United Nations did not fail in the same manner as the League of Nations. The Soviet Union would also be one of the four partners in policing the world. With the allies already policing the world via occupation forces, the formation of the United Nations became Truman's geopolitical priority.

Truman fully supported Roosevelt's plan of charting and organizing the United Nations as soon as possible. During his first speech before a joint session of Congress, held the day after Roosevelt's funeral, Truman confirmed the nation would continue the war with a goal of unconditional surrender, but the nation's focus would be on how to keep the peace after the hostilities.[23] While there was fear, that with Roosevelt's death the San Francisco Conference might be postponed, Truman kept faith with Roosevelt's call for a successful League of Nations in the shape of the UN by stating, "Within an hour after I took the oath of office, I announced that the San Francisco Conference would proceed. We will face the problems of peace with the same courage that we have faced and mastered the problems of war."[24] Throughout his first year, Truman repeatedly supported the UN stating, within his VE Day announcement, the alliance still needed to work hard to defeat Japan and bring about world peace. He further stated the peace effort required as much hard work as was required in war to create a peace environment and the UN.[25] He addressed the Conference in San Francisco affirming his faith in the UN stating, "You members of this Conference are to be the architects of the better world. In your hands rest our future. By your labors at this Conference, we shall know if suffering humanity is to achieve a just and lasting peace."[26] At the Conference's closing in June of 1945, Truman reaffirmed its importance stating, "you have won a victory against war itself with the charter you have completed…this is only a first step toward peace."[27] He further stated, "Out of this conflict have come powerful military nations, now fully trained and equipped for war. But, they have no right to dominate the world. It is the duty of these powerful nations to assume the responsibility for leadership toward a world

---

[22] Offner, *Another Such Victory*, 17.
[23] *Public Papers: Truman, 1945, 3 – 5.*
[24] *Public Papers: Truman, 1945, 4.*
[25] *Public Papers: Truman, 1945, 45.*
[26] *Public Papers: Truman, 1945, 10.*
[27] *Public Papers: Truman, 1945,41.*

of peace."[28] A strong United Nations would be essential to prevent future strife or wars, thereby reducing the need for the nation to maintain a strong, standing army.

The failure of the League of Nations haunted Wilsonian advocates after World War II. Truman, one of those advocates, exerted a great deal of effort as described above to ensure the success of the UN.[29] The world needed a strong, centralized international organization to deter and possibly prevent another world conflagration. As Truman stated, "If wars in the future are to be prevented the nations must be united in their determination to keep the peace under law."[30] Securing world peace, Truman was relying on the UN to allow the United States to reduce the military and thereby cut the military budget. It was a key piece of Truman's strategy in achieving a stable geopolitical environment and thus allowing Truman to balance the federal budget.

Truman also needed a strong United Kingdom to secure the European Continent, thereby allowing the United States to cut its security expenditures. The United States, prior to World War II, had relied on England to not only maintain stability in Europe, but the rest of the world. Due to the costs of World War II, England could no longer maintain its reach or its influence around the world. Truman understood these limitations and the resultant increased responsibility forced upon the United States. In understanding these limitations, Truman was asking England to assume the limited role of supporting and assisting in rebuilding European democracies. With a stable Europe, the United States could reduce force levels and project remaining forces elsewhere.

The last strategic objective of policing the world accomplished two aims. First, the world police would consist of the four major allies: China, Russia, the United States, and the United Kingdom. This joint effort would enhance cooperation and communication among the remaining powers. Secondly, this force, by its very existence, would deter the majority of conflicts or wars throughout the world. The force would be robust enough, if deterrence failed, to counter and resolve the various conflicts that did spring up. This force would also allow the United States to spread the costs of defense among the allies.

---

[28] *Public Papers: Truman, 1945,* 141.
[29] Offner, *Another Such Victory,* 24-25.
[30] *Public Papers: Truman, 1945,* 5.

In addition to securing world peace through the UN, a stable European continent managed by the UK, and a coalition policing the world, Truman sought to reform the world's markets and financial systems. Taking up the ideas of Immanuel Kant's essay *Perpetual Peace*, economic development and international trade were essential to the new world order. Kant tied democracy, free trade, and international governing organization as keys to world peace.[31] Following Kant's concept, Truman supported the Bretton Woods agreement, reciprocal trade agreements, and an international bank focused on economic development. This utopian liberal view was best exemplified by Cordell Hull, former US Secretary of State from 1933 – 1944. He stated, "Unhampered trade dovetailed with peace; if we could get a freer flow of trade...so that one country would not be deadly jealous of another and living standards of all countries might rise, we might have a reasonable chance of a lasting peace."[32] Free trade would create an environment allowing the standard of living to increase in participating nations, a key factor in promoting democracy. Again, Truman's efforts were directed at establishing a more stable, peaceful geopolitical environment that, as a benefit, would allow him to cut military funding.

Truman tied his geopolitical goals along with economic reforms to the ideas of a perpetual peace. With an approach of multilateral agreements encompassing trade, international organization and policing, the United States would be able to reduce its force structure and defense budgets while still ensuring a stable geopolitical environment. Truman had supported President Wilson's ideas following World War I and he was motivated to overcome the hurdles and challenges that blocked the League of Nation's success in creating the new utopian world. Truman's desire to accomplish these goals would color his perceptions with regard to the threat environment.

Threat-Based Model

Of the four models, the threat based budget version should have provided the justification for maintaining a stronger military force than left in 1948. In comparison to force levels in 1940, Truman had cut the army. The threats and actions posed by the

---

[31] Kant, Immanuel, *Perpetual Peace: A Philosophical Sketch.* (1795) http://www.mtholyoke.edu/acad/intrel/kant/kant1 htm (accessed 10 November 2008)
[32] Cordell Hull, *The Memoirs of Cordell Hull, Vol 1* (NY: MacMillian, 1948), 81.

Soviets following World War II should have influenced Truman to restrain demobilization and defense cuts. Instead, while aware of Soviet actions and threats, the Truman administration couched the threats as a political contest of wills and discounted the actual use of military force by the Soviets. Additionally, the nation's atomic bomb monopoly served as an insurance policy in case the administration's threat perception proved false. Truman's focus on the economy and achieving his geopolitical objectives trumped the threats posed by the Soviet Union.

Having been kept in the dark during his days as Vice President, and lacking a strong foreign policy foundation, Truman needed a quick geopolitical tutorial. To accomplish this objective, Truman met with his Secretary of State Edward Stettinius during his first full day as President and requested a report outlining "the background and present status of the principle problems confronting this government in its relations with other countries."[33] The State Department report informed Truman that the United Kingdom's first priority was cooperation with the United States. Churchill wanted to maintain the unity of the three great powers but he was showing "increasing apprehension of Russia and her intentions."[34] The United Kingdom wanted security, but also understood its relative power was declining. Churchill desired to "buttress their position" through Russia and the United States in providing leadership in Western Europe—one of Truman's three geopolitical objectives.

In regards to the Soviet Union, the relationship was not promising, as the report commented, "the Soviet Government has taken a firm and uncompromising position on nearly every major question that has arisen in our relations."[35] During the first four years following World War II, the Soviet Union took a number of actions threatening world peace and the coalition. Stalin created satellite states among the Eastern European nations the Soviets occupied, restricted free elections within Hungary in 1945, and began efforts to take control of Greece and Turkey, between 1945 and 1949, by supporting communist insurgents in each nation.[36] The Soviets had also refused to withdraw forces from Iran. Iran had served as a pipeline for American supplies to reach the Soviet Union,

---

[33] Harry S. Truman, *Memoirs, Volume One Year of Decisions* (Garden City, NY: Doubleday & Company, Inc, 1955), 14.
[34] Truman, *Memoirs*, 14.
[35] Truman, *Memoirs*, 15.
[36] Offner, *Another Such Victory*, 180.

and as such, the Soviets had stationed troops to protect the supply routes. They would finally withdraw these troops in May 1946, only after obtaining oil concessions.[37]

The Soviet Union was also attempting to influence Western European politics by taking advantage of the economic conditions. Even a more direct threat, the Soviets began the blockade of ground resupply routes to Berlin. It would take a massive airlift campaign to thwart Soviet attempts to secure all of Berlin. Lastly, the Soviet Union's successful testing of an atomic bomb in 1949 capped the threat matrix. Yet, through all of these events and continuing threats, Truman continued to cut the defense budget and would not begin to increase defense spending until signing National Security Council Directive 68, and the nation entered into the Korean War.[38] Why was Truman so hesitant to increase the budget, or at least restrain defense budget cuts, given this increasing threat?

Truman was not oblivious to the threats posed by the Soviets and Stalin. As already documented, Truman in 1941 stated that Russia was untrustworthy. However, Truman felt he understood the Russians and in particular, Stalin. Truman commented after his first encounter with Stalin, "I can deal with Stalin. He is honest—but smart as hell."[39] The President felt they were "tough bargainers" asking for everything, expecting just a little.[40] In his memoirs from 1945, Truman further stated, "I could see that there were more difficulties ahead. Already we were at odds with the Soviet government over the question of setting up a truly representative Polish government, and there were troubles in other areas."[41] The State Department report he requested addressed these issues to include the Polish solution, Soviet Union representation at the UN planning conference, and the treatment of liberated areas in Europe. Truman sensed a negative trend and knew the actions during the years immediately following World War II would determine the success of achieving "an orderly world, reasonably secure in peace."[42]

---

[37] Offner, *Another Such Victory*, 118-124.
[38] Offner, *Another Such Victory,* 366-367, 378, 383.
[39] Offner, *Another Such Victory*, 24.
[40] Offner, *Another Such Victory*, 24.
[41] Truman, *Memoirs*, 22.
[42] Truman, *Memoirs,* 22.

His Special Ambassador to Russia, Averill Harriman, who had informed Truman that the world faced a "barbarian invasion of Europe," endorsed Truman's thoughts.[43] Harriman wrote Truman stating "he was convinced Soviet control over any foreign country meant not only that their influence would be paramount in that country's foreign relations but also that the Soviet system with its secret police and its extinction of freedom of speech would prevail."[44] The Russians were not looking to use offensive military actions to acquire territory or additional breathing space. They had already suffered enough bloodshed for a generation. Russian efforts focused on consolidating gains earned during the war, supporting communist political parties in Western Europe, and supporting communist insurgent groups in Turkey and Greece. Due to these facts, the Truman administration's chief fear was not Soviet military strength, but the strength of communist parties and their respective ability to use the economic conditions of a war torn Europe to their advantage.[45] This belief drove Truman to focus on the nation's economy, with even greater emphasis supporting his plan to use the economy's strength to spur Western Europe's recovery and thereby contain communist expansion.

It was important for Truman to believe he could deal with the Russians; he needed this belief to carry on his mission of realizing world peace and achieve his geopolitical goals. These efforts, for Truman, required cutting the defense budget to balance the budget. Truman believed the "only way to establish sound relations between Russia and ourselves was on a give-and-take basis."[46] Truman viewed Soviet intentions as attempts to gain concessions through threat of force, not the actual use of force.

George Kennan, serving as a special advisor in Moscow would also reinforce Truman's action. As Truman sought advice from his administration, Kennan was answering a State Department query that would set the basis for the United States' Cold War strategy. Kennan argued that Soviet actions were not in direct response to American actions; Soviet actions were a result of Russian history and ideological demands.[47] Moreover, he stated there was nothing the West could do to alter this fact. Russia, from a historical perspective, was seeking a greater buffer zone. Russia had suffered numerous

---

[43] Truman, *Memoirs,* 71.
[44] Truman, *Memoirs,* 71.
[45] Roger G. Miller, *To Save a City* (College Station, TX: Texas A&M Press, 2000), 8.
[46] Truman, *Memoirs,* 71.
[47] George Kennan, "The Sources of Soviet Conflict" *Foreign Affairs,* 25, (July 1947), 566-82.

invasions to include Napoleon and Nazi Germany's incursions. From the ideological perspective, the Soviet Union would promote the class struggle supporting communist parties and insurgents around the world. The give and take between the nations was a test of political will.[48] Truman's desire for world peace through a Kantian perspective framed his perceptions of Russian actions. Or at a minimum, Russian actions and intentions were couched in such a way as to validate continued force reductions and minimal defense budgets.

In Truman's geopolitical calculation, the US monopoly with regard to the atomic bomb would serve as an insurance policy in case the nation's threat estimates proved wrong and his international MasterCard to accomplish his geopolitical objectives.[49] The Administration believed the atomic bomb would increase their relative power to "induce the Russians to accede to United States' terms in Germany and contain Soviet gains in Asia."[50] Even more important, Truman believed he had a number of years to push his geopolitical agenda given that his experts had predicted that America's monopoly would last until at least the mid 1950s.[51] This not only gave Truman time to accomplish his strategic geopolitical goals, but for Truman, having the atomic bomb would allow the United States to reduce its conventional force structure; it did not need to match Soviet capabilities in Europe.

The threat-based budget method does provide some understanding regarding Truman's force and budget decisions. With regard to Soviet intentions, Truman's administration chose to believe the Soviets were involved in a test of political wills and would not use force to accomplish its objectives. Truman colored Soviet actions in a positive perspective or at least minimized the threat due in large part to his desire for world peace tied to economic recovery. Even with Soviet attempts to spur communist expansion and refusal to free Soviet occupied Europe, the United States continued to reduce force levels and cut defense funding. Truman had to risk his belief that Stalin would not use force to accomplish Soviet political objectives against the costs of increasing America's force levels. The atomic bomb provided Truman an insurance

---

[48] Kennan, "The Sources of Soviet Conflict" *Foreign Affairs,* 566-82.
[49] Offner, *Another Such Victory*, 97.
[50] Offner, *Another Such Victory*, 97.
[51] Benjamin O. Fordham, *Building the Cold War Consensus: The Political Economy of U.S. National Security Policy, 1949-51* (Ann Arbor, MI: The University of Michigan Press, 1998), 38-39.

policy in minimizing the costs of a strategic mistake, thereby also allowing the reduction of defense expenditures and allowing his focus to remain on the economy. This allowed Truman the time to fix the United States' economy, rebuild Western Europe, establish the United Nations, and create the world police force.

Economy-Based Model

Truman had experienced the Great Depression as a private citizen and as a senator, and these experiences would focus his attention on the economy upon becoming president. Taking his senate seat in 1935, Truman served on the Appropriations and Interstate Commerce Committees, and he gained national attention establishing and chairing the Special Committee to Investigate the National Defense Program, latter called the Truman Committee; his time on the special committee reviewing the defense industry would also give him a good understanding of the economy. [52] His time as an appropriator gave him an understanding of the budget process and this experience would be useful in cutting budgets. During his tenure on the Truman Committee, he demonstrated his bulldog attitude at eliminating fraud and avoiding the waste of taxpayer's money, and this would be evident during his presidency. With all of this experience and perspective, Truman was primed to tackle the economy, and it would be his focus, even though the country was in the midst of war and facing the future threat of Soviet aggression.

Truman believed economic prosperity throughout the world was essential in maintaining a lasting peace. He knew the country had a daunting job ahead in promoting economic prosperity. In a letter to the Director, Office of War Mobilization and Reconversion he wrote, "We still have a tremendous job ahead in bringing the entire war to a victorious conclusion. Beyond that, we must reconvert our domestic economy to the production of peacetime goods and services. The tasks which lie ahead are *no less important, no less urgent, no less vital* to the future of our free institutions than the tasks which are behind us."[53] (emphasis added)

Reaffirming his belief in a strong economy as key to international recovery, Truman sent a letter to heads of the war agencies regarding the European economies. He

---

[52] Offner, *Another Such Victory*, 13.
[53] *Public Papers: Truman 1945*, 29.

addressed the severe food, fuel and logistic support shortages in Europe and that each agency must do all it could to help with the suffering. Truman wrote that "a chaotic and hungry Europe is not the fertile ground in which stable, democratic and friendly governments can be reared."[54] The war had torn Europe apart, destroyed industries as well as farmland. Europe could not support itself. Europeans needed outside aid through those first few winters. In reality, the United States would fight its first battles of the Cold War providing aid to Western Europe. The rebuilding of Europe through the Marshall Plan would be a major part of this endeavor.[55]

For the United States to be in a position to support European needs, the United States had to manage its conversion from a wartime industry to a domestic industrial engine. Throughout 1946 and 1947, Truman encouraged the public and his administration to do all they could to help Europe. He directed the Agriculture Department and National Security Council to direct all of their efforts necessary to maximize wheat production and stated that if the United States did not assist Europe with food and reconstruction, Europe would be unable to help establish peace in the world.[56] He constantly urged Americans to continue growing victory gardens even though the war had ended. Everything Americans could do to reduce consumption and increase production was beneficial to the world and his efforts of securing a lasting peace.[57]

Truman led an aggressive campaign to encourage and motivate American's to work just as hard during the era of peace as it had during the war. At an 8 October 1945 press conference, Truman linked the nation's cultural tendency to demobilize to the economic efforts underway. In answering a question regarding the wave of work stoppages and general labor unrest, Truman answered that everybody felt like letting down. With the great work of winning the war over, Truman needed to motivate Americans to break the nation's tendency to relax and revert to isolationism after war. During a January 1946 radio report to the nation regarding the status of the reconversion program, he stated, "This year we lay the foundation of our economic structure which will have to serve for generations. Decisions will be made whether we want full

---

[54] *Public Papers: Truman 1945*, 61.
[55] Fordham, *Building A Cold War Consensus,* 178.
[56] *Public Papers: Truman 1945*, 96.
[57] *Public Papers of the President of the United States: Harry S. Truman, 1946* (Washington DC: Government Printing Office, 1947), 126.

employment and full production, which will determine if we gain a great future at home and abroad."[58] In this radio address, Truman was pointing out that economic strength at home was the key to peace abroad. The following week, Truman announced the Voluntary Food Conservation program, and he continued calling for conservation of food, maximizing food production, and created an interagency team to assist the UN to stem the world famine. Again, he linked these efforts to the peace process.[59] Truman used the War Power Act to control the economy. To a degree, he waged economic war to control the economy by continuing price and wage controls to control inflation. He did not want a surplus of income to drive up the cost of limited goods, since industry had not fully converted from their wartime footing, it could not produce enough consumer goods to satisfy demand, and Truman worried about the resulting inflationary pressures. Controlling consumer demand was difficult given America had suffered through the Great Depression and had just experienced five years of rationing for the war; Americans now had money and wanted to spend. While his control of the economy was problematic at best, his war against the national debt showed greater results.

Truman was able to send Congress budget reduction requests almost monthly. In August of 1946, Truman informed all executive agencies to reduce expenses in order to reduce the national debt and keep inflation in check. He did not want the government competing for goods in the economy. Truman ordered construction work stoppage, and for agencies to reduce their 1946 budgets.[60] Truman refused to cut taxes until the war was over and the nation honored all of the war bonds. As he cut federal expenditures, the nation began to realize budget surpluses. His efforts were successful with tax revenues exceeding estimates by $4.3 billion and reducing the budget by two billion dollars in 1946.[61] Because of his efforts, Truman submitted a balanced budget for 1948. It was the first balanced budget since 1930.

Truman's drive to balance the budget, to improve and strengthen the economy, influenced the majority of his administration's decisions. For Truman, a strong domestic economy was essential to achieve his geopolitical goals of rebuilding Europe, promoting

---

[58] *Public Papers: Truman 1946,* 1.
[59] *Public Papers: Truman 1946,* 175.
[60] *Public Papers: Truman 1946,* 369.
[61] *Public Papers: Truman 1946,* 196.

democracy, containing Soviet expansion, and maintaining a stable, peaceful world. As such, Truman, with his experience and knowledge gained in Congress, quickly acted to cut the defense budget to balance the budget. The influence of the economic agenda only strengthened the nation's historical norm of quick demobilization and defense budget cuts.

Conclusion

Truman's first full year as President was uncertain, complex, and dynamic. He took his oath while the United States was in the midst of World War II and finalizing its recover from the Great Depression; aptly put, Truman would call his first full year in office as the "Year of Decisions."[62] While he faced serious challenges each year while in office, his first full year would nevertheless set the tone for his administration. Truman had to navigate the United States through the end of World War II, the advent of the atomic age, the conversion from a war to domestic-focused economy, while controlling inflation and unemployment, and creating a stable post war geopolitical environment. The majority of his effort, along with that of his administration team, would focus on the economy. The economy would serve as the nation's foundation to solve domestic issues, ensure the nation's security, and act as the primary means in achieving his geopolitical objectives to include containing communism. This focus would set the tone and drive the administration to an economy-influenced defense budget.

In Truman's view, the threat posed by the Soviet Union was not its military force. Stalin was not ready to start a new war over Western Europe; Russia was busy consolidating its gains from World War II. The communist threat was internal to nations located adjacent to the Soviet Union's borders. Stalin's primary efforts of kicking the allies out of Berlin and supporting insurgents in Greece and Turkey affirmed this view. With the European economies severely damaged, the main threat was from communist political parties taking advantage of the situation and converting the governments internally into communist states. The United States needed to make sure Europe recovered from the ravages of war to block Soviet expansion.

---

[62] Truman, *Memoirs,* 3. Truman titled his first volume of his memoirs the Year of Decisions.

Truman relied primary on American economic power to thwart Soviet aggression. Given his goal was political stability and perpetual peace, the president needed to stabilize Western Europe, as he needed a strong Western Europe to buffer the threat of Soviet aggression, both internal and external. A strong Western European economy would promote democratic governments, prevent communism from gaining a foothold, and provide the capability to build enough military force to deter the Soviet military. If this did not work, America could rely on the power of the atomic bomb.

The four budget models help explain why Truman pulled the defense purse strings tight following World War II despite early signs of Soviet aggression. For Truman, the nation's economy was the essential linchpin to address the nation's future security, to achieve his geopolitical objectives, and to thwart Soviet threats. The cultural behavior of the nation to cut defense forces and funding automatically was only reinforced by Truman's economic focus. As a result, the Army saw its funding drop from $74 billion to six billion dollars in 3 years, while the force structure was cut by 93 percent during that same period.

The end of the Cold War would usher in a new era of peace; but would not result in the same drastic force or funding cuts as the nation had experienced in the past. The Cold War, lasting over 40 years, would actually transform much of the nation's cultural behavior. Economic factors, such as out-of-control deficits, would drive the Bush Administration and Congress to cut defense funding, force levels and programs; but a new cultural norm, New World strategy, and an uncertain threat environment would maintain defense funding and force structure at levels far exceeding those seen during other eras of peace.

Chapter 4

NEW WORLD SAVINGS?

For many, the end of the Cold War signaled the opportunity to cut defense budgets and force structure. The Peace Dividend would allow the nation to balance the budget, and address domestic issues while the Cold War's end would allow for the realization of a Wilsonian world. There were great expectations for the future. Yet, the nation did not cut the defense budget to the levels many expected. Instead, the Bush Administration's new national strategy and threat perspective, while allowing for some force structure and funding cuts, served to support larger than expected defense budgets. Additionally, America's cultural norm of reducing force structure and funding levels to pre conflict levels did not occur. In fact, it appears the Cold War actually transformed the nation's cultural norm to one of embracing a large standing military, enduring deficit spending, and appreciating, or at least accepting, its role as a global power. As expected, economic concerns do provide the reason why the defense cuts were made. Within this chapter, the influence the factors above had on supporting the defense budget decisions following the end of the Cold War will be reviewed.

Is the Cold War Over?

Attempting to date the beginning and the end of the Cold War is problematic. If you gather historians and political scientists together to discuss the topic, the likelihood of developing a consensus on either date is remote. Some experts have submitted the Cold War began as early as the initial "Big Three" meetings while World War II continued to rage or as late as the launching of Sputnik in 1957. Some scholars argue the Russian actions in Poland, Hungary, Greece, Turkey, and the Berlin Blockade served as events pointing to the new conflict. For others, the successful testing of an atomic bomb in 1949 was the wakeup call for the United States. Just as it is difficult to determine the start, dating the ending of the Cold War is just as contentious. The tearing down of the Berlin Wall in 1989 is a commonly accepted event signaling the end of the Cold War. However, this event did not eliminate the threat of a nuclear Soviet Union, and thus end the Cold War. It signaled one crack in the dam holding back the Eastern Bloc's desire for freedom of movement, an increased standard of living, and the reunion of long separated families. These same cracks appeared in Poland with its labor movement, and spread with Gorbachev's reform movements throughout the Soviet Union, the Soviet Union's withdrawal from Afghanistan, and the peaceful transformation from communism to democracy of Eastern Bloc governments. Gaddis likened the Soviet Union and Cold War in 1989 as a sand pile ready to slide; it would just take a few more grains of sand to reach critical mass.[1]

President George H.W. Bush pointed to the events of 1989 as demonstrating the end of the Cold War. Calling it the "Revolution of '89," Bush stated, "I believe we will see this time as the period when much of what the Western democracies sought since the end of World War II *began* to come to fruition."[2] However, there was work left to solidify the gains of 1989. The President ended 1989 meeting with Gorbachev in Malta attempting to do just that. The two leaders used Malta to establish an "ambitious agenda for moving beyond containment towards an era of enduring cooperation."[3]

While the events and Malta did not eliminate the threat of nuclear war, the Cold War threat was diminishing and the future looked bright. But even with this outlook, Bush was not ready to cut the defense budget just yet. His administration was still supporting the funding of the B-2 stealth bomber, Strategic Defense Initiative (SDI), and new mobile nuclear weapons. This support was due to Bush's desire to have as many cards as possible to bargain with as he began to negotiate a new world order and strategic weapon reductions. He repeatedly dismissed calls for cutting defense spending. At various press conferences, the media reported that Congress was beginning to cut defense spending to realize the peace dividend. Bush called for caution and for the nation to wait for a strategic review prior to making cuts. His opinion is captured with this response to a peace dividend stating, "when you mention Peace Dividend, there's almost a –well, there's an uncalled for euphoria in some quarters now that suggests that events where they stand today means that the United States can recklessly—in my view—recklessly

---

[1] John L. Gaddis , *The Cold War, A New History* (New York: Penguin Books, 2005), 238.
[2] *Public Papers of the Presidents of the United States: George H.W. Bush, 1989* (Washington DC: Government Printing Office, 1990), v.
[3] *Public Papers: Bush, 1989*, v.

cut its defense spending. And we are not in that posture."[4] This brings Truman's actions to mind as an opposite example. While Bush was attempting to slow defense cuts, Truman, in stark contrast, was leading the charge cutting the defense budget. Both, however, called for the nation to plan any reduction of defense funding purposefully.

Even though at first he rejected any defense budget cuts in 1989, Bush started cutting the defense budget in 1990 due to economic pressures and attempting to keep his promise of not increasing taxes. While Desert Storm inflated the 1990 and 1991 budgets, the defense budget would go from a high of $538 billion in 1985 down to $358 billion by 1998.[5] The nation had been cutting the defense budget prior to the end of the Cold War. These lower budgets were a reflection of President Reagan's defense build-up during the early 1980s as various major weapon procurement programs were nearing completion by the end of the 1980s. These cuts also responded to increasing deficits and national pressure to control federal spending.[6] While this history helps explain defense cuts prior to 1989, the end of the Cold War, corresponding threat reduction, and the expectation of a peace dividend explain further defense funding decisions.

For some, the cuts during the 1990s were too severe. The nation took a procurement holiday while at the same time reducing research and development funding. The first of several base realignments and closures soon followed. Along with these funding cuts, the force levels went from 2.2 million in 1988 down to 1.4 million in 1998.[7] While for others, the cuts following the Cold War were not severe enough. The budget, overall, was cut by 28 percent; historically, the nation had cut force structure and budgets by over 60 percent within months of conflict termination.[8] Following WWII, for example, Truman cut the budget and force structure by 90 percent. What were the dynamics driving the cuts in the defense budget? Furthermore, what were the factors that impeded deeper cuts mirroring the nation's historical past?

---

[4] *Public Papers: Bush, 1989*, 1603.

[5] United States Department of Defense, *National Defense Estimates for FY2009* (Washington: Department of Defense, 2008), 58-59. $$$ figures indexed to 2009.

[6] Robert D. Hormats, *The Price of Liberty: Paying for America's Wars from the Revolution to the War on Terror* (New York: Times Books, 2007), 242-245.

[7] United States Bureau of Census, *Statistical Abstract of the United States, 2009* (Washington, DC: Government Printing Office, 2009), 322.

[8] United States Department of Defense, *National Defense Estimates for FY2009* . Brevet Maj Gen Emory Upton, *The Military Policy of the United States* (Washington: War Dept, 1912). Both items document the cuts the nation makes following conflicts.

Historical-Based Model

The Cold War reshaped the nation's historical norm of mistrusting standing armies. While Congress had quickly reduced force structure following the conclusion of previous conflicts, the nation was slow to cut force structure and defense budgets following the end of the Cold War. The nation had cut the defense budget and force structure by ninety percent within two years of the end of WWII. The nation, in stark contrast, only cut the defense budget by 28 percent between 1989 and 1998.[9] While a drawdown and budget reductions were expected, these cuts were not automatic nor to the level expected based on the historical norm. There were base closure throughout the United States and overseas along with force reductions. However, the nation did not revert to a force posture or budget proportional to those existent prior to 1949. The defense budget in 1949, relative to 2009 figures, was $182 billion. The smallest budget allocated to the Defense Department during the 1990s was $358 billion in 1998.[10] This was almost double what defense was allocated prior to the Cold War. From these figures, it appears that America had gotten over its distrust of a large military force during the Cold War.

That distrust should have diminished. During the forty years of the Cold War, the military had weaved itself into the fabric of America. There was a greater connection between America and her military. The number of Americans making the military a career significantly increased. Families across the country were more apt to have a service member in their family. Prior to World War II, the average number of citizens serving in the military was 200 thousand, while following World War II, the number fluctuated between two and three million.[11] Additionally, the number of veterans in the nation exploded from an average of four million following World War I to over twenty million after World War II. In 1970, there were twenty-seven million veterans along with three million on active duty within a national population of 200 million—almost 15 percent of the nation had military experience. On top of this, communities viewed their local military bases as local economic engines creating jobs. Colin Powell affirmed this

---

[9] US Department of Defense, *National Defense Estimates, 58-59.*
[10] US Department of Defense, *National Defense Estimates, 58-59.*
[11] Bureau of Census, *Statistical Abstract, 2009,* 342.

belief stating in 1992, "America's armed forces are as much a part of the fabric of US values – freedom, democracy, human dignity and the rule of law—as any other institutional, cultural, or religious thread."[12] Through three generations, the nation had relied on a strong, large military force to win the peace during WWII and maintain relative peace for the forty years of the Cold War. The nation had not experienced a military coup, soldiers were not guarding street corners, and democracy was working. The fears of the Founding Fathers had floundered upon the shoals of the Cold War.

The nation's historical desire to maintain balanced budgets and eliminate debt also does not explain fully the defense budget decisions during the 1990s. Throughout the past sixty years, the nation had repeatedly attempted to balance the national budget and cut the national debt; the records, however, indicate these efforts failed.[13] Presidents Truman and Eisenhower exerted the greatest pressure and budget restraint during their terms. They were the only presidents to actually balance the budget and cut away at the national debt. However, these cuts did not reduce the debt below the levels each inherited. During the forty years of the Cold War, the national debt increased from $252 billion in 1949 to $2.8 trillion in 1989.[14] The nation's debt did stay rather static during the first 25 years of the Cold War; increases were sporadic during the early years. As was to be expected, the Korean and Vietnam Wars did increase the debt. However, the national debt would not exceed $500 billion until 1975. In other words, it would take 26 years for the debt to double. However, the debt would increase exponentially over the next 14 years.

The nation began a pattern of deficit spending to fund both defense and domestic programs during the 1960s. With the combination of Great Society programs and increasing involvement of Vietnam, the United States willingness to assume larger and larger debt to accomplish domestic and security objectives became apparent. How else can you explain a national debt increasing from $500 billion in 1975 to $11.2 trillion in 2009? The nation wrestled with the political problem of whether to raise taxes, incur

[12] Collin Powell, "U.S. Forces: Challenges Ahead," *Foreign Affairs,* Winter 1992/93, 33.

[13] Robert Hormats, *The Price of Liberty* (New York: Times Books, Henry Holt & Company, 2007). Hormats documents the nation's history of raising funds to pay for the nation's wars and pay of national debt, but that a number of administrations failed to cut domestic programs or asked for higher taxes during conflicts such as Vietnam, and Reagan defense build-up.

[14] United States Department of the Treasury, "National Debt Historical Charts," http://www.treasurydirect.gov/govt/reports/pd/histdebt/histdebt.htm.

larger and larger deficits, or cut federal programs. The political rhetoric from both parties described the increasing debt and spending deficits as detrimental to the economy. Even with the rhetoric and some attempts to cut the deficit, the national debt continued to increase. Domestic and security programs, funded from the taxpayer's coffers, had become part of the nation's culture. Although the desire to balance the budget and cut away the national debt existed, its priority became secondary to the economy and national security.

Part of the reason for this focus on national security and maintaining a large defense structure is due in part to a change in the nation's geopolitical view. While generally understood that the nation advocated a position of avoiding foreign entanglements, a closer look at history paints a different picture. The United States, prior to WWII, had chosen a relative isolationist position, and relied on Great Britain to maintain world order. Great Britain, with its formidable navy, secured the oceans, and with its great empire, organized and ruled the mercantile system. The United States took advantage of this construct enjoying the market conditions and paying very little for its national defense. Following the conclusion of WWII, the power of the United Kingdom was spent. The empire no longer possessed the greatest navy nor could it rely on its empire and fund its resurgence. The war had ravaged England and the nation was in debt.[15] The United States was one of two remaining superpowers and had to step into the position left by the United Kingdom. Bush confirmed this change when he stated, within the 1990 *National Security Strategy* document, "In the aftermath of World War II, the United States took on an *unaccustomed burden*—the responsibility to lead and help defend the world's free nations."[16] This became the nation's new norm; the United States became one of the world's superpower and therefore its police officer.

The Cold War transformed the nation's cultural norm. At his inaugural address, prior to the fall of the Berlin Wall, Bush stated, "But the nation had a new history...the US was the world's super power, the benevolent hegemony, had stakes and commitments still in Korea, Europe and soon, the Middle East. It was the nation with largest economy,

---

[15] Walter Russell Mead, *Special Providence: American Foreign Policy and How it Changed the World* (New York: Routledge, 2002), 15-18.
[16] George Bush. *National Security Strategy of the United States 1990-1991*. AFA Book, xv.

the end of the Cold War proved democracy and free trade was the key to success."[17] The nation had to maintain a large military force structure to maintain its role as one of the world's superpower. The country had experienced increasing debt for the past 15 years and the economy continued to grow. Keynesian deficit spending was working. The fears of a standing army, foreign entanglements, and burdensome debt seemed to be baseless.

The nation's new cultural norms, in contrast to the old, were to maintain a strong military, accept deficit spending in an effort to maintain its relative power within the geopolitical environment, and accept global commitments. This was due, in part, to the realization of Eisenhower's feared military industrial complex. The nation and its political leadership were reliant on the jobs created from the local military bases and diverse industrial base further strengthening the new historical norm. The new historical-based model helps explain why the nation did not automatically demobilize and cut defense spending at the end of the Cold War; which was the nation's tendency at the end of wars.

Strategy-Based Model

The nation had taken on the superpower role countering and containing Soviet aggression during the Cold War. With the end of the Cold War, this role was being re-evaluated. There were numerous opinions regarding the nation's direction. Powell believed the nation was obligated to lead, stating, "no other nation on earth has the power we possess. More important, no other nation on earth has the trusted power that we possess."[18] This leadership was based primarily on the nation's armed forces as the "buttress" for the other elements of national power.[19] William Kristol and Robert Kagan warned against the contrasting belief that the time was right for "unshouldering the vast responsibilities the United States acquired at the end of the Second World War and for concentrating its energies at home."[20] They identified different schools of thought coursing through 1990's political discussions.

---

[17] *Public Papers: Bush, 1989*, 1.
[18] Powell, "U.S Forces," 33.
[19] Powell, "U.S Forces," 33.
[20] William Kristol and Robert Kagan, "Toward a Neo-Reaganite Foreign Policy," *Foreign Affairs*, 75, no. 4 (Jul/Aug 96), 18.

These schools included Wilsonian multilateralism and conservative realism practiced by Kissinger disciples.[21] While Kristol and Kagan called for the United States to assume the role of a benevolent global hegemon, the Bush administration was searching for a new strategy and one can find traces of each school. Bush touched on the Wilsonian school while addressing the United Nations in 1989. He emphasized the importance of the UN being a vital forum where nations can seek to replace conflict with consensus and that it must remain a forum for peace.[22] Bush also supported the ideas of promoting economic growth and democracy. He pointed to the successes of Poland and Hungary as examples for the world to emulate.[23] His administration called for reforms in the World Trade Organization and International Monetary Fund that would leverage and support the gains from the end of the Cold War.[24]

The Bush Administration did not push aside Kissinger Realism. While embracing Wilsonian thoughts regarding the geopolitical world, Bush took a pragmatic approach regarding arms negotiations with the Soviet Union. The president continued to demand funding for the B-2, SDI, and additional ICBM platforms to improve his negotiation position. Bush was willing to pursue conventional arm reductions within the European theater because his goal was parity between NATO and the Warsaw Pact. The Warsaw Pact would assume the majority of the cuts and this would allow the United States to redistribute forces. The Soviet Union, even with the thaw of the Cold War, continued to fund and maintain a large nuclear force. Bush wanted to maintain and strengthen America's nuclear forces to be in a more advantageous position during the strategic arms negotiations.

Bush, seeking to continue progress with the Soviet Union, stated he did not want to continue using the term 'Cold War' anymore. His administration predicted progress could be achieved via talks with the Soviets, particularly reducing military arms of all sorts.[25] He agreed there were still uncertainties and problems, and maintained continued reservations regarding Russia. It is within this overall environment that the Bush administration developed the *National Security Strategy* which called for a relatively

---

[21] Kristol and Kagan, "Toward a Neo-Reaganite," 18.
[22] *Public Papers: Bush, 1989,*1248 – 1252.
[23] *Public Papers: Bush, 1989,* 896.
[24] *Public Papers: Bush, 1990,*161-165.
[25] *Public Papers: Bush, 1989,* 22.

large military force and defense budget.[26] This is very similar to Truman requesting the State Department to provide an intelligence overview of the geopolitical environment in 1945. The revised strategy did not call for large defense budget cuts; it called for more of a reallocation of defense funding to meet a full spectrum of threats.

The *1990 National Security Strategy's* (NSS) elements consisted of protecting the safety of the nation and its citizens, creating a sense of community with those nations sharing our values, and a commitment to a free and open global market.[27] While these were enduring elements were linked to the nation's history, the strategy's objective of maintaining the ability to project power around the world was based on the nation's new role as the world's superpower. Each of these elements or goals influenced the funding and maintenance of the nation's defensive structure.

The nation, according to the Bush Administration, could not exist in a world full of dictators.[28] To continue its existence, the nation had to continue promoting democracy around the world. This was a break from the Jeffersonian foreign policy concept of looking internally and promoting democracy from America's shoreline. Under this Jeffersonian construct, American democracy should serve as a beacon for the world. Attempting to promote and export democracy countered this philosophy. A number of the security strategy's objectives lined up with this goal. These included actions to stabilize and secure the world, foster political freedom, and stabilize regional military balances to deter regional dominance. This overall direction required the nation to maintain a strong military force and continue its forward presence. Powell, within his 1992 article, reinforced this idea stating peacekeeping and humanitarian operations were a given as future military operations in the future.[29] It would be these types of operations along with stabilization missions that would assist the exportation of democracy.

The promotion of free trade, by reducing trade barriers and championing open international trade, has long been an American political objective. Rooted in both Hamiltonian and Wilsonian foreign policy schools, these schools view free trade as a key

---

[26] *Public Papers: Bush, 1989*, 22.
[27] Bush, *National Security Strategy*, 3.
[28] Bush, *National Security Strategy,*4.
[29] Powell, "U.S. Forces: Challenges Ahead," 36.

to supporting democracy.[30] According to these schools of thought, free trade enhances local, regional, and global markets. This trade encourages market growth around the world increasing the standard of living among cooperating nations; as the water rises, all ships rise. As a nation's standard of living increases, its ability to adopt democratic forms of government increases.[31] In addition to improving the chance for other nations to become democratic, free trade ensures access to foreign markets, thereby enhancing America's economy. For Hamilton, a healthy US economy was necessary to ensure opportunities for individual prosperity and provide the resource base for national endeavors.

The objective of maintaining a global position, with the ability to project force throughout the world, underwrote the NSS first two elements of promoting democracy and free trade. Given the first two goals are linked closer to a Wilsonian construct, the third element reflects a more pragmatic approach. This element required the nation to maintain forces in Korea, Japan, throughout Europe, and in multiple other locations. This new philosophy was demonstrated repeatedly during the 1990s as the nation opposed Iraq's invasion of Kuwait, and conducted operations in Panama, Central America, Somalia, and Bosnia, to name a few. The nation required the force structure to project power to maintain stability throughout the world. The final goal was also tied to national survival. The nation's ability to project power helped to deter aggression and end conflicts on favorable terms. This capability was necessary to counter the new threat environment.

The end of the Cold War required the nation to rewrite of its nation security strategy. No longer directly concerned with Soviet aggression, the nation began to promote Wilsonian and Hamiltonian ideas of free trade, democracy, and collective security. These new objectives did not allow for a huge reduction of defense budgets. The Bush administration took a pragmatic approach to its relations with the Soviet Union and other threats. It wanted to reduce conventional weapons, but also sought additional funding for strategic programs. The nation increasingly focused on terrorism and failed

---

[30] Mead, *Special Providence: American Foreign*. Mead, within his book, reviews and examines the four schools of political thought throughout the nation's history and how the Hamiltonian and Wilsonian schools promote trade, democracy and collective security, although for different reasons.
[31] Bruce Russett and John Oneal, *Triangulating Peace* (New York: W.W. Norton & Company, 2001), 72.

states. Bush wanted to take defense funding and reallocate it within the department to address these new threats. He did not readily accept the concept of a peace dividend.

Threat-Based Model

The threat of a nuclear holocaust faded with the ending of the Cold War. Yet while the world seemed to breathe a sigh of relief regarding a war between the super powers, the proliferation of nuclear weapons along with biological and chemical weapons possessed by failing states continued to threaten the world. The peace expected from the end of the Cold War mutated into a world of new and expanding threats. The erosion of the bipolarity permitted and, in many ways, encouraged the growth of conflict and the proliferation of WMD and ballistic missiles.[32] In this changing environment, the United States began to switch its focus from the global threats posed by Soviet Union to a regional focus on threats from terrorism, failed states, and regional conflicts. This switch was constrained by a continuing uneasiness regarding the Soviet Union, and later, the Russian Federation.[33] Due to the uncertainty and complex environment, the Bush administration was very reluctant to cut defense funding. Bush again preferred to reallocate funding and develop a force structure based on a capabilities construct to address a full range of threats.

The United States had primarily built its defense capabilities based on the threat of the Soviet Union. As Powell stated, "When we were confronted by an all-defining, single, overwhelming threat—the Soviet Union—we could focus on that threat as the yardstick of our strategy, tactics, weapons and budget."[34] But as the Cold War faded into history, Bush was not willing to simply dismantle military capabilities determined by the Soviet threat. The Soviet Union still possessed the same military capabilities as it did the day before the Berlin Wall fell. It might have lost the manpower and equipment possessed by its Warsaw Pact members and their commitment, but it still held the overwhelming edge in terms of conventional forces on the European Continent.

The threat environment at the end of the Cold War contrasted starkly to the threat environments at the end other US conflicts. This difference is exemplified by comparing

---

[32] Bush, *National Security Strategy*, 21.
[33] Bush, *National Security Strategy*, 32-35.
[34] Powell, "U.S. Forces: Challenges Ahead," 41.

the end of World War II and the Cold War. At the conclusion of World War II, the Axis powers' ability to wage war had been destroyed. The allies had sought and obtained the unconditional surrender of Japan and Germany. The characterization of the Soviet threat following World War II allowed the United States to begin a drastic drawdown of forces. The conditions were in stark contrast at the end of the Cold War. Each nation still maintained the same relative level of capabilities. The end of the Cold War allayed fears about Soviet intentions, not the capabilities. Bush had to take steps to address and reduce the capabilities of both sides to have a chance to realize any savings.

During July of 1989, the Bush administration continued NATO's efforts to address capabilities by offering a proposal to cut conventional force levels in Europe. Bush believed that positive movement within Eastern Europe (moving toward economic growth and free elections) required the drawdown of conventional forces on both sides. He actually stated the cuts could go further and be more sustainable if they were linked with political change.[35] These cuts would result in matching tank, artillery, and aircraft strength between the two alliances. It would set manpower ceilings of 275,000 per each side and require the demobilization of remaining forces and destruction of excess equipment.[36] This agreement greatly benefited the West since it evened the score regarding conventional forces. These cuts began to take shape by the latter months of 1989. Brent Scowcroft, Bush's national security advisor, responding to a foreign press member's question during a presidential press conference, stated that the Soviets had reduced some of their conventional forces, and therefore, probably were cutting their defense spending. He followed up that statement by indicating the Soviet Union had not reduced their spending or attention on strategic forces and this was still a concern.[37]

The President would echo Scowcroft's statement during the 1990 State of the Union Address. In addressing the "Revolution of 1989" as marking the beginning of a new era, Bush cautioned Congress regarding defense cuts stating, "we are in a period of great transition, great hope, and yet great uncertainty. We recognize that the Soviet military threat in Europe is diminishing, but we see little change in Soviet strategic modernization. Therefore, we must sustain our own strategic offensive modernization

---

[35] *Public Papers: Bush, 1989,* 921.

[36] *Public Papers: Bush, 1989,* 653.

[37] *Public Papers: Bush, 1990,* 214, 686.

and SDI."[38] The threat was declining in regards to intention. As to capabilities, it remained problematic and Congress needed to address this issue by supporting the nation's own strategic weapons program. This justified continue spending on SDI, the rail garrison peacekeeper and smaller ICBM platforms along with the B-2 stealth bomber. During a session with reporters discussing the 1990 defense budget, Bush stated the nation needed these programs to ensure it had "the utmost flexibility in terms of arms control."[39] When asked why the nation was spending $70 billion on a bomber and not addressing the nation's infrastructure needs, Bush responded that his prime responsibility was the national security of the United States.[40]

While the diminishing Soviet threat became clearer, allowing the United States to reduce its force levels and budget, the threats from regional powers and failed states continued to grow in complexity and uncertainty, which required forces and funding to address. When the media asked Bush about the future of NATO and the Warsaw Pact, he stated he could not predict what would happen in the next ten days much less ten years.[41] The world was increasingly complex. Within the *1990 National Security Strategy,* a number of new threats either were recognized or received greater attention. The document recognized that with the erosion of the United States and Soviet bipolar world, that there would be an increase in third world conflicts. The super powers would no longer contain nationalism as it spread through the world.

In terms of capabilities, the world would see a greater diffusion of weapon production increasing the availability of various weapons to smaller nations. This would reduce the military gap between hostile nations, eroding any deterrent capability then existing. Within this environment, the United States might find it more difficult to react. Threats posed included terrorism, the war on drugs, upheaval of regional stability, a rising China, and weapons such as integrated air defense systems, WMD, and ballistic missiles.

The diminishing threat from the Soviet Union and new threats posed by terrorism and failed states pulled on the nation's purse strings seeking sustained funding. Congress

---

[38] *Public Papers of the Presidents of the United States: George H.W. Bush, 1990* (Washington DC: Government Printing Office, 1991), 133.
[39] *Public Papers: Bush, 1989,* 1003.
[40] *Public Papers: Bush, 1989,* 1003.
[41] *Public Papers: Bush, 1989,* 1589.

and budget hawks were demanding defense cuts in light of the Cold War's end. The Bush administration and defense hawks were cautioning against funding cuts and proposing reallocation of defense budgets. Bush stated he did not want to "cut into the muscle of the military," that with the threat diminished in Eastern Europe, the United States would require a "rapidly deployable force."[42] Within the State of the Union Address, Bush decoupled America's military presence in Europe from the Soviet threat by stating, "that an American military presence in Europe is essential and that it should not be tied solely to Soviet military presence in Eastern Europe."[43] The justification for a large military force, forward projected, began to be based on the new threat environment by 1990.

The Cold War threat had justified maintaining a large military complex and its required funding. As was to be expected, the nation's natural inclination was to demand drastic defense cuts once the Cold War ended. However, the termination of the Cold War did not have any historical parallels. In terms of threats, only the intentions of the Soviet Union diminished. The Soviets retained their capability to wage war even as the Iron Curtain fell. Even though Bush was able to reduce conventional forces, reducing strategic forces still held challenges for him. With the erosion of the bi-polar world, new threats had emerged requiring his attention and the nation's funding.

As the only superpower remaining, the United States was saddled with addressing these new threats. For the Bush Administration, cutting the defense budget based solely on the demise of the Soviet Union was not advisable. His administration agreed that some cuts could be realized, but the cuts had to be surgical and not cut into the muscle of the military.

This revised threat environment does provide some explanatory power of why the nation did not follow its natural tendency to revert to force and funding levels prior to the conflict's beginning. Nevertheless, the reduction in the threat level because of the Cold War ending allowed the nation to actually grasp the purse strings; defense funding was no longer off-limits. Concerns with the economy and deficit spending provided the impetus to close the purse.

---

[42] *Public Papers: Bush, 1990*, 100-101.
[43] *Public Papers: Bush, 1990*, 132.

Economy-Based Model

Besides revitalizing the nation's defensive structure, President Reagan also introduced the concept of Reaganomics to revitalize the nation's economy. The nation during the 1970s had experienced, as President Carter described it, a malaise resulting from high inflation rates, equally high unemployment, and the national debt closing in on one trillion dollars.[44] Reagan promised that his economic reforms would reawaken the nation and spur its recovery and growth.

President Bush, during the 1980 Republican debates had described Reagan's plan of trickledown economics as "Voodoo Economics." Nevertheless, Reaganomics did seem to have fulfilled its promises. As Bush entered the presidency, the nation was still experiencing its longest peacetime economic expansion in history. The economy had created over 20 million jobs since 1982, checked inflation, and had experienced 83 months of continuous growth. This was the status as 1989 began; but there were signs the economy was facing challenges as the nation entered the 1990s.

Bush faced the challenges of balancing the federal budget, cutting the national debt, keeping tax rates static, and ensuring economic prosperity. Each of these challenges would pressure him to reduce the defense budget and apply the savings to accomplish domestic goals. Bush was faced with the age-old problem of balancing defense spending and domestic spending. The pressure to resolve these problems pushed Bush to enact defense-funding cuts.

The nation crossed the trillion-dollar debt threshold during 1982 and was approaching a debt level of four trillion dollars by 1992. As stated earlier, the nation had taken almost 25 years to double the national debt from $250 billion to $500 billion. Now, the nation was doubling the debt level every two and half years. The nation needed to control its deficit spending. Bush recognized this need when, during a press conference in 1989, he stated the nation still needed to make progress reducing the deficit and ultimately reduce the nation's debt.[45] He bemoaned the fact Congress was not supporting his 1990 Federal Budget. The 1990 budget would have reduced the deficit to less than

---

[44] States Treasury Department, "National Debt Historical Charts, 1789 - 2009," http://www.treasurydirect.gov/govt/reports/pd/histdebt/histdebt.htm.

[45] *Public Papers: Bush, 1989,* 962, 1099, 1123.

$100 billion; but Congress added additional spending to the budget. Even though the economy was growing, Bush believed the nation needed to cut the deficit to keep the economy growing.[46] Again, during a press conference in January 1990, Bush stated that if he could get Congress to help reduce the deficit, that those cuts would help the fundamentals of the economy.[47]

A majority of Americans believed the nation could cut the defense budget to help balance the budget.[48] Kristol and Kagan confirmed this statement stating the "American public is more interested in balancing the budget than in leading the world, and more intent on cashing in the peace dividend than on spending to deter and fight future wars."[49] Bush supported the concept of balancing the budget and again linked its accomplishment to the health of the economy during his 1990 State of the Union Address.[50] He even agreed that any savings from the defense budget should be applied to the national debt.[51] However, he again cautioned any defense cuts by stating, "it would be imprudent to make reckless cuts in our defense and think everything was just perfect in the world. It isn't."[52] The threat environment served to constrain Bush from making defense cuts in 1989. Bush had to find another method to address the deficit.

Bush had famously run his 1988 election campaign on the promise not to raise taxes. By stating, "Read my lips, I will not raise taxes," he handicapped his administration's ability to raise additional revenue to address the nation's deficit concerns. This election promise created additional tension between maintaining the defense budget and balancing the budget. Without the ability to raise taxes, Bush had one less option to address either problem. Was national security as measured by defense expenditures more important than the campaign promise? As already pointed out, Bush contended his role was to ensure the nation's security; that this role was of greater importance than domestic programs.

---

[46] *Public Papers: Bush, 1989*, 1446.
[47] *Public Papers: Bush, 1990*, 80.
[48] Steven Kull, *Americans on Defense Spending – A Study of US Public Attitudes: Report of Findings*, (Washington: Program on International Policy Attitudes, 1996), 6.
[49] Kagan and Kristol, "Toward a Neo-Reaganite Foreign," 19.
[50] *Public Papers: Bush, 1990*, 131-132.
[51] *Public Papers: Bush, 1989*, 1673.
[52] *Public Papers: Bush, 1989*, 1673.

The Bush administration also understood the connection between the defense budget and the economy. While savings from defense funding cuts could help reduce the deficit, thereby improving the economy, those same cuts could also harm the economy. Between 1989 and 1991, over 1.6 million jobs were lost as the nation reduced its force structure by 431,000; defense industry lost 400,000 and an additional 800,000 jobs were lost from the non-defense sector.[53] Bush understood that by cutting the defense budget, he was also cutting jobs across the nation.

While Congress supported defense cuts in order to enjoy peace dividend returns, this same Congress continued to support Cold War weapon systems. This support might have been couched in terms of national security, but the primary reason for Congressional support was jobs.[54] The loss of jobs was even more acute in regions with base closures. During another press conference, the media asked about the impact of defense cuts and base closures. Bush responded by stating, "the key is to maintain a strong private economy so private investors can move into these areas and spur the local economy."[55] For Bush, the nation needed a strong economy in order to support defense cuts and base closures. For the economy to be strengthened, the nation needed to cut the budget deficit.

The economy model provides the best explanation why the nation cut defense funding. While the lessening of threats due to the end of the Cold War allowed defense funding to be considered for funding cuts, it was the nation and the Bush administration's perception that national debt and increasing annual deficit spending was weakening the economy that drove the actual cuts. Bush had taken tax increases off the table during his election campaign, which left only federal budget cuts to solve the deficit problem. The defense budget represented the largest section of the discretionary budget; and with the end of the Cold War, it was the simple solution. While Congress and others were calling for larger and larger cuts, Bush attempted to hold back the tide. Bush was focused on his role of ensuring the nation's security, and while understanding cuts to the defense budget could lower the budget deficit, he understood defense cuts hurt the economy by cutting

---

[53] Powell, "U.S. Forces: Challenges Ahead," 43.

[54] Thomas Cardamone, " Cold War Relics: Why Congress Funds Them," *Foreign Policy In Focus,* 5, no 29 (Sept 2000), 1.

[55] *Public Papers: Bush, 1990,* 100-101.

jobs. This reluctance to cut defense funding drastically led Bush to break his promise and increase taxes. It was within this tension that cuts were made to the defense budget.

Conclusion

The United States celebrated and rejoiced with Europe as the Iron Curtain fell. Not only was the threat of nuclear annihilation thrown off and the freedom of millions from communism realized, the nation entertained the eternal hope of cutting the defense budget and finally reducing its debt. The nation's debt was soon to exceed $4 trillion, increasing by $3 trillion over the past decade. The economy, although having experienced the longest peacetime expansion, showed worrying signs of decline and a possible recession. The lessening of the forty-year threat seemed to open the door to cut defense funding and resolve other domestic problems.

The four budget formulation perspectives provide explanatory power to explain why the nation did not drastically cut its defense budget. First, the Cold War transformed the nation's cultural norm. The nation no longer seemed to distrust a large standing army, grew to accommodate budget deficits supporting preferred security and domestic programs, and accepted its role as the world's lone superpower. Its prior cultural norm was in stark contrast. Had the nation followed its tendencies prior to the Cold War, the nation would have cut defense funding by over 60 percent. During the decade following the Cold War, the nation only cut its defense funding by 28 percent. The historical construct, in light of the Cold War's influence, explains why the automatic response was not to cut the defense budget.

Linked to the cultural norm was the nation's new strategic outlook. Instead of relying on the oceans to protect the nation from invasion and the United Kingdom to rule the mercantile system, the United States had to assume its own security and develop policies promoting global free trade. Instead of providing the world a beacon for democracy, the nation sought ways to export its form of government. The nation also continued to push Wilsonian and Hamiltonian concepts of international organizations, and free trade. The nation's strategy required the maintenance of a strong defense structure able to project forces around the world.

It needed a force to address the new threat environment. These new threats, including WMD, ballistic missiles, terrorism and regional conflicts, required flexible forces able to address two possible conflicts at once. Bush also required funding for strategic forces to ensure a strong position with pending strategic arms negotiations. Both the threat and strategic perspectives supported maintaining a strong military force and large defense budgets.

The economic model is the best construct that explains why the nation made cuts to the defense budget. Bush fought defense cuts stating his primary role was to ensure national security; however, he was also concerned with the economy. He felt that a key to a strong and growing economy was a balanced federal budget. Given that he had refused to raise taxes, defense-funding cuts were the primary way to cut the deficit. The nation would cut the force structure by over 400,000, close bases, and reduce the annual budget by roughly 40 billion dollars. But, due to the nation's new historical norm, strategic goals and regional threat environment, the nation did not cut defense funding as drastically as would be expected. Bush, due to this tension of reducing the deficit to strengthen the economy and ensure the nation's security, would finally raise personal taxes thereby breaking his election promise and harming his re-election in 1992.

Chapter 5

STUDYING THE PAST TO SOLVE THE PROBLEMS OF TODAY

The Obama administration's Fiscal Year 2010 Federal Budget promises a "New Era of Responsibility" while "Renewing America's Promise." To fulfill the promise of transforming the economy and establishing a new foundation for long-term economic growth and prosperity during these difficult times, Obama must examine the policies and decisions of previous administrations that faced similar circumstances.

President Obama faces serious problems spanning the nation and the world. The nation's economy is in a downturn with a six percent reduction in overall growth during the last quarter and the loss of over six million jobs during the past year.[1] The budget, set at over $3.5 trillion, increases the nation's debt by $1.75 trillion to record levels.[2] The nation faces, along with economic worries, a resurgent Russia, two ongoing wars, the proliferation of WMD, global terrorism, and the threat of world unrest due to worsening economic conditions. Along with these challenges, Obama is facing a possible pandemic, the collapse of the financial infrastructure, the demise of the United States auto industry, and continuing global environmental concerns. Any one or two of these problems would challenge the energy and skills of any previous national government; Obama's administration faces multiple challenges.

It is against this backdrop that the Obama administration must determine how much to spend for national security. As this thesis has pointed out, the problem of balancing limited resources while ensuring the nation's security and economic prosperity has confronted the nation since its birth. In confronting this recurring problem, the nation must answer a myriad of questions regarding the defense budget as addressed in chapter two. In answering these questions, the nation, and more importantly, the administration must understand the various factors that influence the decision process.

---

[1] United States, Bureau of Labor Statistics, "Employment Situation Summary, April 2009," *Economic News Release,* http://www.bls.gov/news release/empsit.nr0.htm (accessed 1 June 2009)

[2] Rebecca Christie, "Geithner Tells China U.S. Will Tackle Budget Deficit," *Bloomberg,* 1 June 2009, http://www.bloomberg.com/apps/news?pid=20601087&sid=aFaYiMwPZyq0&refer=home (accessed 1 June 2009).

As stated before, the nation cannot purchase absolute security, no matter the size of the budget, knowledge of the threat environment or the perfection of strategy. In light of these limits, the nation charges the strategist with developing a strategy and defense budget that limits the potential errors and their effects on the nation's security. During the nation's first 150 years, the cultural norms of avoiding foreign alliances, maintaining a small military, and financial conservatism kept defense funding at a minimum during eras of relative peace. The nation took advantage of its geographic location, and a world ruled by the United Kingdom to keep defense costs low and marginalize strategic errors. In response to a direct threats of war, the nation was willing to mortgage the economy to secure the nation's freedom.

This thesis' purpose was to review the defense-budget decision process of the Truman and Bush administrations. In particular, how each administration examined and responded to the various external factors in determining the amount to allocate to defense. The budgeting models, linked to the factors, used in the case studies helped to explain the actions each administration took. These models, to include historical-based, economy-based, threat-based, and strategy-based, did help explain the actions of the administrations.

Although a good starting point in building the defense budget, the historical-based method is too simple. The method is disconnected from emerging threats and a changing geopolitical environment. Arguments promoting increases or decreases in defense spending based on past budgets are simplistic. The method does help the strategist understand the nation's culture when attempting to radically cut or reallocate defense budgets. The historical model demonstrates how the momentum of cultural norms' can influence the process.

While the threat-based method does address the security environment, the method can be problematic. A strategist, attempting to justify budgets based on opponent capabilities, is prone to engaging in a competition to build the most powerful weapons, and this competition then drives the budget. Attempting to determine the opponent's intentions is difficult. The threat-based method also focuses the strategist attention to the more obvious threats, thereby blinding him to new and emergent threats. The method does focus the nation's budget attention to the capabilities needed to secure the nation.

While surely a restraint to the overall budget, the economy-based argument can be fraught with challenges. The nation cannot link the defense budget to a certain percentage of GDP or limit the budget to what remains after funding domestic priorities. This process is also simplistic and does not guarantee security. The economy-based budget does consistently close the nation's purse string.

The strategy-based method is the best in developing a defense budget. By conducting a detailed analysis in developing the nation's geopolitical objectives, the strategist can better prepare a budget that can accomplish those objectives. The objectives serve as a beacon while the threats and economic conditions of the nation serve as constraints. However, the strategy-based method does not provide the best explanation of why the nation cuts or does not cut defense budgets following the nation's conflicts.

As the nation emerged from World War II, the geopolitical environment was transformed by the atomic bomb, expansion of communism, and the unrecoverable degradation of the United Kingdom's power. The threats posed by the Soviets were couched in terms of economic conditions and as a contest of political wills; for Truman, the Soviets did not pose as a military threat in the short term. Therefore, instead of maintaining a military to match Soviet conventional military capabilities, Truman chose a strategy closely linked to Wilsonian and Kantian concepts of world peace, and focused his efforts to sustain and improve the nation's economy. A threat-based budget approach to justifying larger defense budgets was trumped by the nation's historical-based response at the end of conflicts, the Wilsonian-based strategy, and most importantly, Truman's drive to improve the economy by balancing the federal budget. Truman focused and relied on the nation's economy to accomplish both his domestic and geopolitics objectives. As a result, the nation cut its force structure and defense funding by 90 percent within 18 months following World War II.

In stark contrast, Bush, after fighting to maintain the defense budget, proposed a defense budget that would cut funding by just 28 percent over the ten years following the Iron Curtain's fall. As the curtain fell, the demise of the Soviet threat allowed the defense budget to be considered for further funding cuts, while economic concerns of the early 1990s would actually pull the nation's purse strings and motivate the cuts that were made. However, why were the cuts not deeper or similar to those experienced following World War II?

The nation's new historical norms, new threat environment, and new geopolitical strategy served to keep defense funding at a higher level than expected. While the threat of a superpower spurred nuclear war had diminished, the new threat environment was not benign. In fact, the threat environment became more problematic, chaotic, and uncertain resulting in calls to reallocate defense funding instead of cutting defense. This new threat environment of terrorism, WMD, and ballistic missile proliferation provided the impetus to maintain larger defense budgets than expected at the end of a conflict. In addition to the threat environment change, the nation's new cultural norms explain why the nation did not cut defense funding as deeply as expected.

The Cold War transformed the nation's historical norm of mistrusting standing armies, avoiding foreign entanglements, and financial conservatism, each having influenced the nation to cut defense funding in the past. The nation's new role as a superpower, global alliances, requirement for large forces, and deficit spending behavior during the Cold War had gathered a momentum of their own. This momentum and new cultural norms supported larger defense expenditures than expected from reviewing the nation's history. Lastly, the nation adopted a geopolitical strategy that required a large, flexible force able to respond to multiple regional conflicts.

The Obama administration can identify with many of the same challenges Truman and Bush faced—an ailing economy, record debts, uncertain threat environment, and need for a new or modified national security strategy. Similar to Truman, Obama inherited a two front war, although limited, faces an uncertain threat environment, and must resolve record debt and deficits. With regard to the Bush administration, Obama inherited the cultural norms resulting from the Cold War, the political momentum sustaining large defense budgets.

Like both Presidents Truman and Bush, Obama is pressured by economic concerns to cut the defense budget to reduce the 1.2 trillion dollar budget deficit; a deficit Obama promises to cut in half by the end of his first term. Unlike its size during Truman's term, the current defense budget represents a minority share of the total federal budget, and if domestic programs were untouched, would have to be completely eliminated to accomplish Obama's goal. As a result, Obama will have to prioritize the nation's objectives and make tough choices to cut the deficit.

Within those tough choices, the Obama administration must determine the context of the threat environment. It is true that the administration will need a sense of its political objectives to identify potential threats, but the combination will assist its efforts. The manner in which Obama couches the possible threats of a rising China or resurgent Russia will heavily influence his defense budget decisions.

Lastly, the strategy he chooses to address these threats will bear directly on his funding decisions. If he chooses to approach the world and nation's problems from a Wilsonian perspective reliant on diplomacy and economics, this will translate into smaller defense budgets. With the recent use of military in Iraq and Afghanistan, and respective results, it is unlikely Obama will use the military for other than relief efforts or to counter a direct attack.

It appears from this review that the historical-based model is the primary support for maintaining large defense budgets. The budget's momentum, its job creation capability, and political support for bases and pet projects serve to prop up the budget. On the other hand, the nation's economic condition and the administration's apparent diplomatic focused geopolitical strategy may call for and support cuts to the defense budget. These cuts might not cut the deficit in half, but they would be a start.

The wildcard, as it was to a degree during the Bush administration, are the threats perceived and recognized. If the 2010 defense budget, the appointment of Ashton Carter (a proponent of cutting Cold War weapons, as the Undersecretary for Acquisition, Technology and Logistics), and recent comments by Defense Secretary Gates are any indication, the threats from a rising China or resurgent Russia will be discounted. The Administration has cut many of the conventional-war acquisition programs and is reallocating funding to programs most likely to be employed in today's fight.

Given this framework, Obama will need to construct a case based on economic concerns, a new threat environment evaluation and his strategy to confront and challenge the momentum of the defense budget. By linking funding to his national strategy, the administration will be best able to achieve its objectives.

Bibliography

Brodie, Bernard. "Strategy as a Science," *World Politics* 1, no. 1 (1948), 467-488.

Brodie, Bernard. *Strategy in the Missile Age*. Santa Monica: Rand Corp, 1959.

Bush, George. *National Security Strategy of the United States: 1990-1991 (An Ausa Book)*. Washington, D.C.: Brassey, Inc, 1990.

Bush, George. *Public Papers of the President of the United States, 1989*. Washington: United States Government Printing Office, 1990.

Bush, George. *Public Papers of the Presidents: George Bush, 1990*. Washington: United States Government Printing Office, 1991.

Cardamone, Thomas A. Jr, "Cold War Military Relics: Why Congress Funds Them" *Foreign Policy In Focus,* 5, no. 29 (September 2000): 1. http://www.foreignpolicy-infocus.org/ (accessed 9 November 2008)

Carter, Ashton. "Defense Strategy & Budget in the Post Bush Era." Belfer Center Programs or Projects – Preventive Defense Project (5 August 2008) http://belfercenter.ksg.harvard.edu/publications/18521/defense_strategy_budget_i n_the_post_bush_era (accessed 9 November 2008)

Christie, Rebecca. "Geithner Tells China U.S. Will Tackle Budget Deficit." *Bloomberg,* 1 June 2009, http://www.bloomberg.com/apps/news?pid=20601087&sid=aFaYiMwPZyq0&ref er=home (accessed 1 June 2009).

Department of the Army. *Annual Report of the Secretary of the Army, 1948*. Washington: Government Printing Office, 1949.

Department of Defense, *Annual Report of the Secretary of the Army, 1948,* Washington: Government Printing Office, 1948.

Department of War. *Report of the Secretary of War to the President, 1921*. Washington: Government Printing Office, 1921.

Department of War, *Report of the Secretary of War for the Year, 1890*. Washington DC: Government Printing Office, 1891.

Dolman, Everett. *Pure Strategy: Power and Policy in the Space and Information Age*. New York: Routledge, 2005.

Feldstein, Martin. *The Economic Stimulus and Sustained Economic Growth,*

Fordham, Benjamin O. and Thomas C. Walker. "Kantian Liberalism, Regime Type, and Military Resource Allocation: Do Democracies Spend Less?" *International Studies Quarterly*, 49 (2005) 141-157.

Fordham, Benjamin. *Building the Cold War Consensus: The Political Economy of U.S. National Security Policy, 1949-51*. Ann Arbor: University of Michigan Press, 1998.

Foster, John Bellamy, Hannah Holleman, and Robert W. McChesney. "The U.S. Imperial Triangle and Military Spending," *Monthly Review.* (October 2008) http://www.monthlyreview.org/081001foster-holleman-mcchesney.php (accessed 9 November 2008)

Gaddis, John Lewis. *Strategies of Containment: A Critical Appraisal of American National Security Policy during the Cold War*. New York: Oxford University Press, USA, 2005.

Gray, Colin S.. *Explorations in Strategy*. Westport, Connecticut: Praeger Paperback, 1998.

Gray, Colin S.. *Fighting Talk: Forty Maxims on War, Peace, and Strategy*. Westport, CT: Praeger Security International General Interest-Cloth, 2007.

Gray, Colin S.. *Modern Strategy*. New York: Oxford University Press, USA, 1999.

Heller, Charles and William Stofft, ed. *America's First Battles: 1776 – 1965*. Lawrence, KS: University Press of Kansas, 1986.

Hetrick, Ron L. "Employment in High-Tech Defense Industries in a Post Cold War Era" *Monthly Labor Review* (August 1996) http://findarticles.com/p/articles/mi_m1153/is_n8_v119/ai_18749025 (accessed 9 November 2008)

Hitch, C.J. *Economic Aspects of Military Planning,* Santa Monica, CA: Project RAND, 1956.

Hoover, Herbert. *The Hoover Commission Report on Organization of the Executive Branch of Government*. New York: McGraw-Hill Book Company, 1949.

Hormats, Robert D.. *The Price of Liberty: Paying for America's Wars from the Revolution to the War on Terror*. New York: Times Books, 2008.

Hull, Cordell. *The Memoirs of Cordell Hull, Vol 1*. NY: MacMillian, 1948.

Isenberg, David. "The US Military's Fallout Shelter." *CATO Institute* (8 October 2008) http://www.cato.org/pub_display.php?pub_id=9702 (accessed 9 November 2008)

Jervis, Robert. *Perception and Misperception in International Politics*. Princeton: Princeton University Press, 1976.

Johnson, David E. *Fast Tanks and Heavy Bombers: Innovation in the U.S. Army, 1917-1945*. Ithaca, NY: Cornell University Press, 1998.

Johnson, Wray R. "Whither Aviation Foreign Internal Defense?" *Airpower Journal* XI, no. 1 (Spring 1997): 66-86. http://www.airpower.maxwell.af.mil/airchronicles/apj/apj97/spr97/johnson.pdf (accessed 20 Mar 08).

Kant, Immanuel. *Perpetual Peace: A Philosophical Sketch*. (1795) http://www.mtholyoke.edu/acad/intrel/kant/kant1.htm

Kennan, George. "The Sources of Soviet Conflict," *Foreign Affairs,* 25, (July 1947): 566-82.

Krepinevich, Andrew F. *The bottom-up review: An assessment*. Washington DC: Defense Budget Project, 1994.

Kristol, William and Robert Kagan. "Toward a Neo-Reaganite Foreign Policy" *Foreign Affairs*, 75, no. 4 (July/August 1996): 18-32.

Kull, Steven. *Americans on Defense Spending – A Study of US Public Attitudes: Report of Findings*, Washington: Program on International Policy Attitudes, 1996.

Lewis, Gaddis John. *The Cold War: A New History*. New York: Penguin Press HC, The, 2005.

Linn, Brian McAllister. *The Echo of Battle: The Army's Way of War*. Cambridge, MA: Harvard University Press, 2007.

Marshall, George C., *Biennial Reports of the Chief of Staff of the United States Army to the Secretary of War: 1 July 1939 – 30 June 1945,* Washington, DC: Government Printing Office, 1965.

Mead, Walter Russell. *Special Providence: American Foreign Policy and How it Changed the World.* New York: Routledge, 2002.

Miller, Roger G.. *To Save a City.* College Station, TX: Texas A&M Press, 2000.

Moltke, Helmuth, Graf Von and Hughes, Daniel J. *Moltke on the Art of War: Selected Writings.* New York: Presidio Press, 1995.

Muravchik, Joshua. "NATO's Impact on Democratic, Economic Institutions." American Enterprise Institute, October 1997. http://usinfo.state.gov/journals/itps/1097/ijpe/pj4murav.htm (accessed 9 November 2008)

Murtha, John, Congressman. Address. Center for American Progress, Keynote Address, Washington DC, 10 December 2008.

Nitze, Paul. "The Grand Strategy of NSC-68." Address. National War College, Washington DC, 20 September 1993.

Offner, Arnold. *Another Such Victory: President Truman and the Cold War, 1945-1953.* Stanford : Stanford University Press, 2002.

Oneal, John, and Bruce M. Russett. *Triangulating Peace: Democracy, Interdependence, and International Organizations.* New York: W. W. Norton, 2001.

Posen, Barry R. *The Sources of Military Doctrine: France, Britain, and Germany between the World Wars.* Ithaca, NY: Cornell University Press, 1984.

Pollin, Robert and Heidi Garrett-Peltier. *The U.S. Employment Effects of Military and Domestic Spending Priorities,* Dept of Economics and Political Economy Research Institute: University of Massachusettes-Amherst (October 2007).

Powell, Colin L. "U.S. Forces: Challenges Ahead" *Foreign Affairs,* (Winter 1992/93): 32-45.

Project on Defense Alternatives, *The Paradoxes of Post-Cold War US Defense Policy: An Agenda for the 2001 Quadrennial Defense Review,* 5 February 2001, http://www.comw.org/pda/0102bmemo18.html (accessed 9 November 2008)

RAND Review, "Future Defense Budgets: A Skeptic's View" (Fall 1997) http://www.rand.org/publications/randreview/issues/RRR.fall97.QDR/future.html (accessed 9 November 2008)

Robb, Charles S. "Rebuilding a Consensus on Defense" *Parameters* (Winter 1996-97). http://www.carlisle.army.mil/USAWC/parameters/96winter/robb.htm (accessed 9 November 2008)

Rosen, Stephen Peter. *Winning the Next War: Innovation and the Modern Military.* Ithaca, NY: Cornell University Press, 1991.

Russett, Bruce and John Oneal. *Triangulating Peace.* New York: W.W. Norton & Company, 2001.

Schelling, Thomas C. *Arms and Influence.* New Haven, CT: Yale University Press, 1966.

Sharp, Travis. "Pentagon Budget Faces Uncertain Future: Momentum Accelerates for Reform; Budget Cuts Possible." Center for Arms Control and Non-Proliferation (15 April 2008) 3 February 2009. http://www.armscontrolcenter.org

Sharp, Travis. "Tying U.S. Defense Spending to GDP: Bad Logic, Bad Policy" Center for Arms Control and Non-Proliferation (15 April 2008) http://armscontrolcenter.org/policy/securityspending/articles/tying_spending_to_g dp_bad_policy (accessed 9 February 2009).

Smith, Rupert. *The Utility of Force: The Art of War in the Modern World.* New York:

Vintage, 2008.

Stevenson, Charles A.. *Congress at War: The Politics of Conflict Since 1789*. Chicago: Potomac Books Inc., 2007.

Tiron, Roxana. "Murtha: Defense Spending under Severe Pressure." *The Hill,* 10 December 2008. http://thehill.com/index2.php?option=com_content&task=view&id=78226&pop=1&page (accessed 30 December 2008)

Truman, Harry S.. *Public Papers of the Presidents of the United States: Harry S. Truman, 1945*. Washington: Government Printing Office, 1961.

Truman, Harry S.. *Memoirs, Vol 1 Year of Decisions*. New York: Doubleday, 1955.

United States, Bureau of Census, *Statistical Abstract of the United States, 2009*. Washington, DC: Government Printing Office, 2009.

United States, Bureau of Census. *Historical Statistics of the United States, Colonial Times to 1970*. New York: Basic Books, 1976.

United States, Bureau of Labor Statistics. "Employment Situation Summary, April 2009." *Economic News Release,* http://www.bls.gov/news.release/empsit.nr0.htm (accessed 1 June 2009)

United States Department of Defense, *National Defense Estimates for FY2009* Washington: Department of Defense, 2008.

United States Treasury Department, "National Debt Historical Charts, 1789 - 2009," http://www.treasurydirect.gov/govt/reports/pd/histdebt/histdebt.htm.

Upton, Emory. *Military Policy of the United States*. New York: Government Printing Office, 1916.

Waterman, Shaun. "Budget Analysts Warn of Spiraling Defense Spending." *Washington Times* (12 February 2009) http://ebird.osd.mil/ebfiles/e20090212656650.html (accessed 12 February 2009).

Watson, Mark Skinner. *Chief of Staff: Prewar Plans and Preparation*. Washington, DC: Department of the Army, 1950.

White House, "Obama's State of the Union Address, 2009," http://www.whitehouse.gov/the_press_office/remarks-of-President -Barack-Obama-Address-to-Joint-Session-of-Congress/ (accessed 5 March 2009)

Wolk, Herman S. "Strategic Deterrence: the Fragile Balance." *Air University Review* (July-August 1976). http://www.airpower.maxwell.af.mil/airchronicles/aureview/1976/jul-aug/wolk.html